D0416750

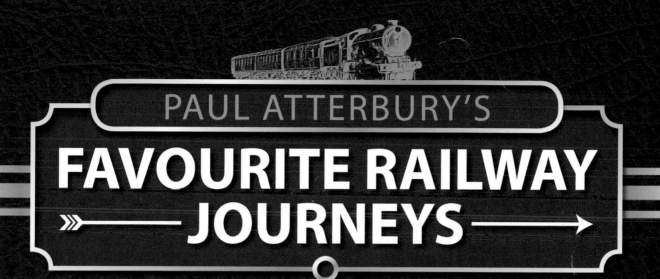

PAUL ATTERBURY'S
FAVOURITE RAILWAY
JOURNEYS

PAUL ATTERBURY'S

FAVOURITE RAILWAY
JOURNEYS

D&C

David and Charles

CONTENTS

INTRODUCTION

For many people train travel is just a necessity, a quick and efficient means of transport that tends to be taken for granted, until it goes wrong. Yet, a train journey can be so much more, bringing together history, landscape and the particular but ever-changing view of Britain through the carriage window. Much of the network in use today, and its infrastructure, is a legacy of the 19th century, built by Victorian entrepreneurs and engineers determined to overcome all of the challenges they faced. Their achievement was colossal, and they built a 20,000 mile railway system whose tentacles reached into the distant corners of the British Isles. The modern network is much smaller, having been steadily reduced between the 1920s and the 1970s, with the main cuts following the publication of Dr Beeching's report in 1963.

The fifty years that have passed since Dr Beeching have witnessed massive changes, both to the national railway network itself, and in the way that railways are perceived. Several unexpected things have happened. First, more passengers travel on the modern railways than were carried by the much larger network that operated before the Beeching cuts. Second, the heritage railway industry has grown massively, bringing both nostalgic pleasures and economic growth to many remote corners of Britain. The steam train experience is widely available, and very popular. Third, railway travel today can be more about the journey and its route than the purely practical business of getting from A to B. Rail tours flourish and quiet country routes are frequently marketed as enjoyable tourist experiences.

Fourth, while the modern emphasis is on high speed main line and suburban commuter traffic, there has been an increasing awareness of the value of secondary and country routes, both in social terms and as contributors to tourism.

These secondary and country routes were, of course, the main target for Dr Beeching, compelled as he was by a government firmly committed to road transport to make railways pay. There were significant losses, particularly for branch lines and other lesser routes hard to justify in purely economic terms and there is, as a result, a widespread belief that not much of value remains. This book aims to change that, by showing that country railways and branch lines are still operating in many parts of Britain, offering the kind of exciting and visually stimulating journey traditionally associated with the pre-Beeching era.

The routes selected for this book are particular favourites, with a special combination of landscape, history and visual pleasure. They range from short, but classic, branch lines to long-distance routes that explore some of the best of Britain's countryside to link interesting cities, towns and villages. The journeys are arranged regionally, from the far west of Cornwall to the Highlands of Scotland. They also represent the full history of Britain's railways from the 1850s to the early years of the 20th century.

Apart from the routes themselves, and the engineering achievements they encompass, the most important legacy of the railway age is the railway station. There was no such thing as a railway station until the first one was opened in 1830, but from that point it became one of the most familiar buildings of the Victorian era. Inventive, practical and stylistically diverse, the railway station was at the social and economic heart of Victorian Britain. Thousands were lost during the Beeching period, but over 2,000 are still in use, ranging from huge city termini to remote country halts. Stations and station scenes are part of the great panorama of the railway experience and luckily they have been well documented by generations of railway photographers, both professional and amateur, whose images are used throughout this book to document these favourite journeys.

This book is aimed primarily at the armchair traveller. However, it is hoped that readers will be encouraged to leave their armchairs to explore the wonderful railway journeys that are still there to be enjoyed all over Britain's national railway network.

SOUTHWEST ENGLAND

Station Scenes

The railways of the Southwest were interestingly varied. The few main lines supported a dense network of rural routes and branch lines, and there were numerous small stations serving country towns and villages, many of which have closed since the 1950s. Traffic was mixed: passenger services were busy during the holiday season, while regular goods trains carried vegetables, fruit, flowers and other agricultural produce, minerals and local freight throughout the year. A number of coastal resorts in Cornwall, Devon and Dorset depended on the railways, both major West Country services, such as the daily Cornish Riviera and Atlantic Coast expresses to and from London, and the many local trains. A selection of stations in these counties, along with some in Somerset, feature on these pages.

▲ The line to Ilfracombe, a heavily graded 14-mile branch from Barnstaple, was opened in 1874 and in due course became one of the destinations for the Atlantic Coast Express. Here, in the 1960s, passengers disembark from the local stopping train while mailbags are loaded and unloaded.

◄ It is a quiet, hazy day in the summer of 1962 at Penzance. Two long trains await their passengers and a GWR Class 6800 locomotive, No. 6845, 'Paviland Grange', slowly backs towards some wagons.

▲ Steam and diesel meet at Torrington, on the Devon line south from Barnstaple Junction and Bideford. There seem to be no passengers, and closure, in 1965, is not far off. Today the station survives as a pub and the line is a cycle track.

▲ Petrockstow was one of a number of rural stations in North Devon, on the remote line from Torrington to Halwill Junction. Despite handsome stone buildings, there was never much traffic.

▼ The sidings at Okehampton often saw military traffic, for exercises nearby. Here, at some point before World War I, horse teams are being assembled. The horses have been delivered to the station by train, together with men and equipment.

▲ At Halwill the LSWR's meandering north Cornwall line met the branch to Bude and the line south from Torrington, to be seen branching away at the top of the photograph. Until the late 1950s this was a busy place, but little survives today.

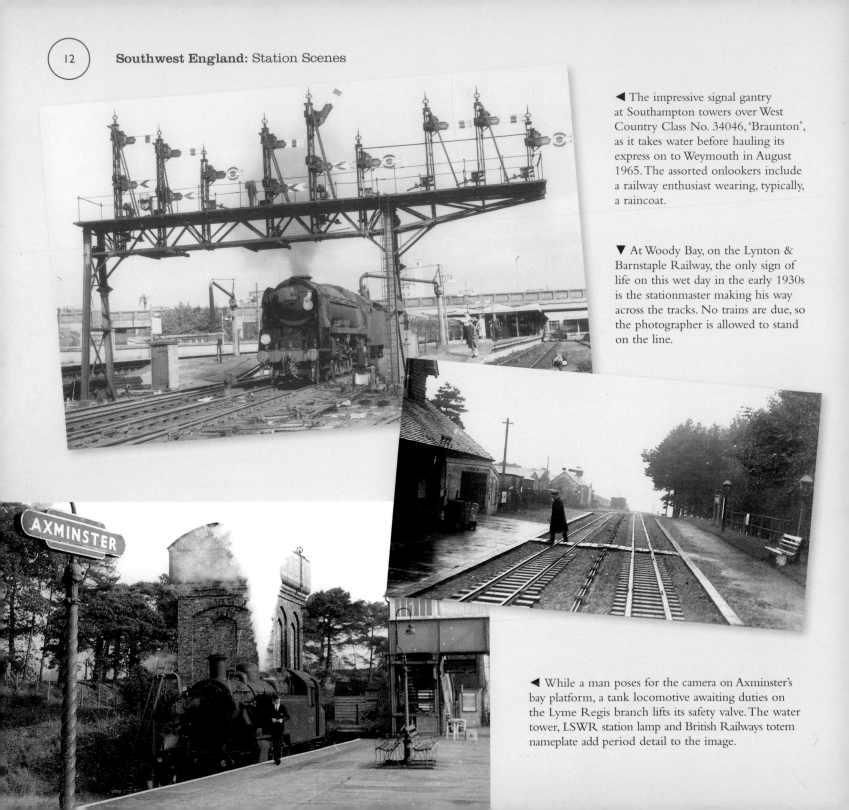

◄ The impressive signal gantry at Southampton towers over West Country Class No. 34046, 'Braunton', as it takes water before hauling its express on to Weymouth in August 1965. The assorted onlookers include a railway enthusiast wearing, typically, a raincoat.

▼ At Woody Bay, on the Lynton & Barnstaple Railway, the only sign of life on this wet day in the early 1930s is the stationmaster making his way across the tracks. No trains are due, so the photographer is allowed to stand on the line.

◄ While a man poses for the camera on Axminster's bay platform, a tank locomotive awaiting duties on the Lyme Regis branch lifts its safety valve. The water tower, LSWR station lamp and British Railways totem nameplate add period detail to the image.

► This Edwardian view shows Midsomer Norton station on the Somerset & Dorset Joint Railway. The decorative paintwork, milk churns ready for collection and ladies in smart hats off on a shopping trip or visiting friends, make a lively scene.

S&D. JUNCTION RY STATION MIDSOMER NORTON 13985

▼ At Weymouth in the 1950s the Channel Islands ferry has docked and the train is ready to depart along the quay tramway, with a Class 5700 tank engine in charge. Three men chat with the driver while, to the left, a couple are deep in conversation beside their elegant Triumph saloon.

▲ Two men and a boy have adopted a deliberately casual pose at Moorswater, near Liskeard, the only passenger station on the clay line from Coombe to the quarries at Caradon and Cheesewring.

POOLE: RAILWAY GATES, HIGH STREET. 41437.

▲ The regular passage of trains through the level crossing on Poole's high street still, today, brings everything to a halt. This Edwardian card shows not much has changed over the last hundred years.

▶ A Class 45 diesel draws a train from Newcastle into Bristol Parkway station in the summer of 1972. Staff and passengers walk to meet it, watched by children in a Cardiff-bound train on the other platform. Mineral wagons fill the sidings.

▼ The station is deserted, but all is neat and tidy. The trolleys are stacked and the old iron LSWR signs have been carefully repainted in this classic 1950s summer scene.

TICKET OFFICE

▲ The Gothic style of Bristol Temple Meads makes it one of Britain's most distinctive stations. The typically Victorian blend of Tudor and French motifs in two-colour stone was designed by Matthew Digby Wyatt and completed in 1878. This photograph shows the building in 1973, soon after a full and careful restoration.

◄ A porter halts his passage across the tracks for the photographer in this moody view of Bristol Temple Meads, taken perhaps in the 1920s. Behind him, the 4-4-2 tank is ready to depart, and in the background the station walls are covered in advertisements.

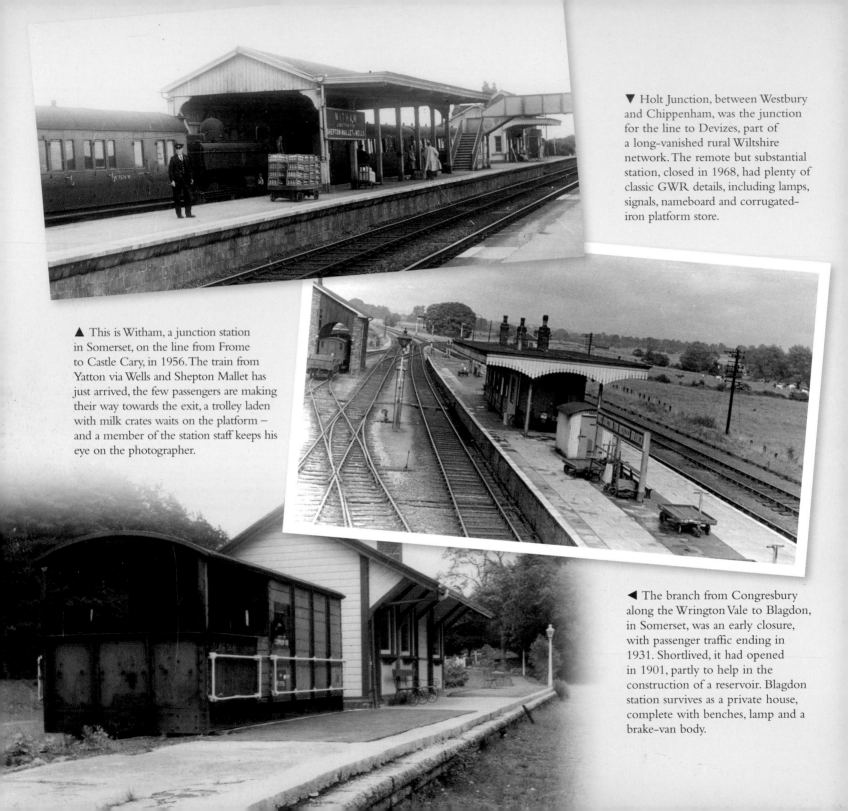

▼ Holt Junction, between Westbury and Chippenham, was the junction for the line to Devizes, part of a long-vanished rural Wiltshire network. The remote but substantial station, closed in 1968, had plenty of classic GWR details, including lamps, signals, nameboard and corrugated-iron platform store.

▲ This is Witham, a junction station in Somerset, on the line from Frome to Castle Cary, in 1956. The train from Yatton via Wells and Shepton Mallet has just arrived, the few passengers are making their way towards the exit, a trolley laden with milk crates waits on the platform – and a member of the station staff keeps his eye on the photographer.

◀ The branch from Congresbury along the Wrington Vale to Blagdon, in Somerset, was an early closure, with passenger traffic ending in 1931. Shortlived, it had opened in 1901, partly to help in the construction of a reservoir. Blagdon station survives as a private house, complete with benches, lamp and a brake-van body.

▶ In this early 20th-century view of Camerton station, the posing staff are rather upstaged by the line of wagons laden with the products of the Somerset coalfield. Milk churns indicate the more usual traffic on the branch – which in the 1950s became famous as the setting for the filming of *The Titfield Thunderbolt*.

▼ Pewsey is a rare survivor among rural Wiltshire stations. Here, in July 1975, a Class 50 diesel brings the Paddington-to-Paignton train into the platform while a small huddle of passengers – some quite possibly setting off for a Devon holiday – wait to board.

Liskeard to Looe

With railways to St Ives and Looe, Cornwall can justly claim two of the best surviving branch lines in Britain. While tourism has kept the St Ives branch open, the mainstay of the Looe line has been the clay industry. Quarries and clay were what built the line early in the 19th century, and it is the clay from Moorswater that keeps it going. Its origins were in two mineral lines, the Liskeard & Looe Railway, opened in about 1828, and the Liskeard & Caradon Railway, opened in 1844; both had connections with the much earlier Liskeard & Looe Canal. Until 1901, when the present link with the main line at Liskeard station was completed, the railways had little interest in carrying passengers. However, this new link encouraged the development of both the port at Looe and tourism, and since then the journey to Looe by train has been a popular experience.

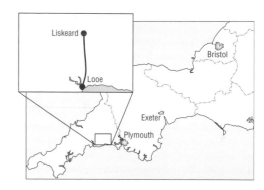

The real branch line experience

At Liskeard, the train for Looe leaves from what is in effect a separate station, an old timber building set to one side. From here it plunges 200 feet, curving under the great viaduct that carries the main line. At Coombe it joins the old Moorswater line, where it has to reverse. Those in the know turn to face the other way, so the best of the route is still ahead. The journey is a series of delights, passing through woods and flower-filled fields, closely following the river and its tidal estuary. Birds, boats and the occasional remains of the old canal add to the appeal. It is a remote and leisurely journey, a constant reminder of the nearly extinct pleasures of true branch line travel. Looe station is outside the town, but the ride makes up for this minor inconvenience.

▼ Looe is divided by the river into two parts, East Looe and West Looe, linked by the road bridge. The railway is on the east side, just visible in the distance on this Edwardian postcard. Also apparent are the two quays, busy with fishing boats and coastal trading vessels, some of which would have engaged in the clay trade. Fred, writing on the front of the card, told his friend Ernest in Bradford, that he 'had a peep at this spot on Saturday'.

◄ Beyond Sandplace, where boats in the sand trade used to load at the head of the estuary, the track runs along the river shore. This section of the journey is a complete contrast to the earlier passage through woods and fields. The views are wonderful, as is the birdlife on the estuary at low tide. Modern railcars, like this one, make excellent viewing platforms.

◄ A journey on the Looe branch is rich in old-fashioned railway experiences. Here the guard has got out of the train to change the points at Coombe Junction, where the train reverses. The train itself may be modern, but the old branch line atmosphere lives on.

◄ Until the 1960s Looe was a busy place, with some freight as well as passenger trains. The line used to extend beyond the station to the East Quay, to serve the harbour. In this 1950s photograph the locomotive has pulled the train clear of the station in order to run round it for the return journey. There is none of this today, and the distant station buildings have been replaced by a minimal shelter and a single track.

Bristol to Weymouth

The Beeching axe was very thorough in its reduction of Britain's railway network in the 1960s, but there were some surprising survivors. One such is the line from Bristol to Weymouth, a meandering and predominantly rural route that must have looked like a prime candidate for closure. Somehow it escaped and is now one of the best country railways in England, offering a leisurely exploration of some of the more secret parts of south-western Britain.

Linking Somerset, Wiltshire and Dorset, the line has a long history, its route having been planned by the Wiltshire, Somerset & Weymouth Railway in 1845. This grandly named company was nominally independent but its backer was the GWR, keen to gain access to a south coast port, and thus to French and Channel Islands' traffic. It was planned from the start as a broad-gauge line, part of Brunel's ever-expanding empire, and the first section opened in 1848.

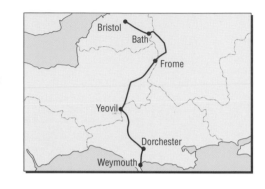

▶ There is no tram to be seen in this 1930s view of Tramways Centre, at the heart of Bristol, but it is full of period detail. Traffic is somewhat lighter than today, but otherwise the scene is still recognizable. The gothic splendour of Temple Meads station is a suitable starting point for a notably old-fashioned journey. The train usually departs from a platform resplendent with the stylish cream and brown GWR ceramic signage of the 1930s.

TRAMWAYS CENTRE, BRISTOL

37592

► A stopping train from Salisbury to Bristol, under the control of a GWR Hall locomotive, pauses at Bradford-on-Avon in 1963, having joined the Bristol to Weymouth line at Westbury. For much of its life, this route was kept busy with traffic generated by its various connections with other main lines. Typical were the summer holiday expresses that linked Weymouth directly with the Midlands and the North via this route.

▼ The ubiquitous modern diesel railcars operate the Bristol to Weymouth service today, but sometimes in the summer longer locomotive-hauled trains are used to cope with the holiday traffic. This view of the train passing Claverton Weir, near Bath, shows the quality of landscape associated with the route.

▼ Frome's timber 1850 train shed, a direct link with the time of Brunel, survives thanks to the mainline bypass of 1933. It is now a unique example of a once-common GWR station type.

Things then began to go wrong and construction was constantly delayed by difficulties and financial problems. In 1851 the GWR ran out of patience and took over what remained of the WS&WR, finally completing the line in 1857. It remained a broad-gauge route until 1874, and in 1884 it was converted to double track. By 1876 the GWR was operating shipping services from Weymouth. Apart from access to Weymouth harbour, there were other advantages for the owners, and thanks to its connections with main lines at Westbury (for GWR West Country services), Bruton (for the Somerset & Dorset) and Yeovil (for the LSWR's West of England routes), it was increasingly used by freight and holiday traffic.

▼ At Castle Cary the Weymouth train leaves the GWR main line for the now single-tracked route southwards through the hills of Dorset, a notably remote region where stations that elsewhere would have closed years ago survive as request stops.

SOUTHERN RAILWAY. 787
TO
FROME
G.W.R.

The journey

Today the line offers a delightful journey of great landscape diversity, with plenty of interesting things to see en route. Elements reflecting Brunel and the GWR survive and many stations are old-fashioned in atmosphere. Some are request stops, so passengers wanting to board the train have to stand on the platform and wave. Those on the train have to ask the guard in advance to arrange for it to stop. Old semaphore signals are still in use in some areas, and other echoes of past railway life are to be seen.

The journey starts from Bristol Temple Meads and the train follows the main line to Bath before turning south along the Avon valley to Bradford. It crosses the wide, open Wiltshire landscape to Trowbridge and Westbury, a windswept station dominated by the massive stone traffic from nearby quarries. The next stretch is along the GWR main line to Exeter, via Frome, Bruton and Castle Cary, where the Weymouth line turns south through the gentle hills and farmland of Somerset to Yeovil, a town that has two of its original three stations still in use, albeit not connected by scheduled services. The train now enters the glorious and remote hill country of Dorset, running south through villages redolent of Thomas Hardy and over the territory of once-famous hunts to Maiden Newton, formerly the junction for the branch line to Bridport and West Bay, another creation of the GWR's south coast harbour ambitions.

▲ In the 1950s a long Weymouth-bound holiday train, headed by a GWR Hall locomotive, waits at Yeovil Pen Mill station. Journey's end is now in sight for weary passengers who have travelled for hours from the north of England. At this point there were connections for Yeovil's other stations, Town and Junction. With semaphore signals intact, Pen Mill looks remarkably similar today.

◄ As so often in early 20th-century postcards, everyone is posing for the camera. This is Maiden Newton in about 1910. The station is not greatly changed today, except that it now has no staff and not many trains. To the left of the footbridge was the bay platform for the Bridport branch, a line that somehow kept going until the mid-1970s.

Maiden Newton, Railway Station

▼ The line from Weymouth to Dorchester, used by both GWR and SR trains, was heavily graded, so double-heading was common. Here, in the summer of 1939, as war clouds were gathering, a long express crawls past Upwey Wishing Well Halt.

Dorchester, another two-station town, is approached through Poundbury tunnel, which was dug instead of a cutting, on Brunel's orders, to preserve the Iron Age earthworks above. In Dorchester the rails of the GWR and the LSWR come together, to share the final few miles down to Weymouth. The two lines opened on the same day in 1857, a reflection of the cooperation between the two companies that continued until the era of British Railways. From Weymouth they built a joint extension to serve Portland, initially for both broad and standard gauge, and there were equally equitable arrangements about the use of the Weymouth harbour tramway, whose route through the town centre to the quayside ferry port was in use until the late 1980s. In its heyday Weymouth, the meeting point for all kinds of GWR and SR locomotives and vehicles, was a trainspotter's dream.

▼ The Weymouth harbour tramway was a delightful anachronism and until its closure in the late 1980s trains wound their way through the traffic and the holidaymakers. It was built to serve the ferries to France and the Channel Islands, and in this typical 1960s view a boat train of SR stock, hauled by a GWR tank locomotive, sets off along the crowded quayside towards the town centre. Perhaps those on the train have taken part in one of the excursions advertised in the booklet on the right.

▼ Weymouth has been a resort since the 18th century, thanks to its harbour and sheltered sandy beaches, but it was the railway that really made the town famous. This Edwardian card gives the flavour of the beach, complete with bathing machines.

DAY EXCURSIONS
By sea
FROM WEYMOUTH

CHANNEL ISLANDS
Guernsey and Jersey
FRANCE Cherbourg
No Passport

1962

SOUTHERN
BRITISH RAILWAYS

Weymouth. The Bay.

ALES & STOUT

WH 109

Station Architecture

Gothic and Tudor

The great architectural debate of the 19th century was Gothic revival versus classical. Through the century the battle ranged widely and continuously, without clear winners or losers. The new Palace of Westminster was Gothic, the Foreign Office classical. The debate also divided the railway builders but they added a new regional angle with the north and north-west of England favouring the classical camp, while Gothic was more associated with the south of England, the Midlands, East Anglia, Wales and Scotland. Gothic was a very fashionable style indeed in the first part of the 19th century, and was at its peak from the 1830s to the 1870s. It was successful because it represented a sense of history, Christianity, wealth and extravagance, industrial and imperial success, and a strong element of patriotism. Gothic was above all else perceived as a suitably British style. To the Victorians, Gothic meant a number of things, including medievalism, Tudor, Jacobean and many aspects of the traditional vernacular, in fact anything that was not overtly classical. As a result, it could also incorporate European elements, notably Flemish, French, German and Italian. As a new building type, the railway station was a reflection of its age. It gloried in the stylistic confusion that Gothic and Tudor represented, but still saw it as eminently suitable for the new railway buildings of the modern age, combining history and permanence with new technology. It was also flexible, applicable alike to city termini and to country halts.

▲ There are many famous Gothic stations but few can compete with Bristol Temple Meads. Brunel was not a natural Goth, but his original 1840 terminus, to the left of the present station, flew the Gothic, or Tudor, flag. This set the pattern for the 1878 station, a glorious and extravagant structure with its famous central clock tower.

◄ This 1930s panoramic view of Gilbert Scott's majestic 1870s Midland Grand Hotel at St Pancras shows railway Gothic at its most imaginative and ambitious. With this building the Midland Railway put itself firmly on the map.

▲ This 1910 picture of Brading, on the Isle of Wight, shows the simplest possible use of Gothic, with arched windows added to a plain brick building.

▼ When completed in 1848, Brocklesby station, in Lincolnshire, was described as 'a very chaste erection in the pure Elizabethan style'. It was an ambitious building by the Manchester, Sheffield & Lincolnshire Railway and, although closed, survives.

▲ The North Staffordshire Railway was adventurous in its architecture, favouring a decorative Tudor style that was the speciality of its chosen architect, Henry Hunt. Typical is Stone, built in 1849, a perfect small-scale exercise in the style, featuring careful symmetry, contrasting brick and stone, Flemish gables and tall, decorative chimneys. Recently restored, Stone is a fine memorial to local ambition and elegance.

▲ For country stations Brunel created a simple cottage style with Tudor and vernacular overtones, including hipped roofs or well-defined canopies. This drawing shows Twyford, in Berkshire, in the 1840s.

Classical and Italianate

Dominant through the 18th century, the classical style had lost some of its appeal by the start of the railway age, partly because it was perceived by many to be pagan and thus unsuitable for a Christian country. However, its formal grandeur and elegance appealed to some early railway tycoons, mainly because it represented power, stability and permanence. For this reason, classicism was popular with northern industrialists, and therefore with some railway builders in the north of England. Conventionally symmetrical and adhering to the rules and orders laid down by the architecture of Greece and Rome, classicism was used in the Victorian period with considerable freedom. Styles of the ancient world featured alongside the classicism of the Renaissance, and in many cases were adapted for different materials. The building that set the standard for the pure classical style was Philip Hardwick's great portico for Euston, wantonly destroyed in the early 1960s. This was echoed in Birmingham and in many other places but, at the same time, a more informal and relaxed classicism was developed for railway stations that simply drew in a general sense upon Italianate and Renaissance models. By this means, stations great and small all over Britain could be called classical in a general way, and this tradition was maintained well into the 20th century, with some fine 1920s and 1930s neo-Georgian examples.

▲ Completed in 1850 by the LNWR and Lancashire & Yorkshire Railway, Huddersfield is Britain's most magnificent classical station. A mass of columns, colonnades and pilasters, it has the look of a grand country house.

◄ With a style determined by the city it served, Bath Green Park, seen here in 1959, is a pure statement of classical symmetry. Built by the Midland Railway, completed in 1870 and closed in 1966, it was the link between the industrial north of England and the south coast.

Central Railway Station, Nottingham.

◀ Nottingham's Central, or Victoria, station was only loosely classical, reflecting as it did a mix of French and Italian Renaissance elements. Completed in 1900, it was closed in 1967 and subsequently demolished, leaving only the clock tower to survive as a famous city landmark.

▶ G T Andrews, a close associate of George Hudson, the 'railway king', designed many stations for the York & North Midland Railway and developed a characteristic domestic style of Italianate classicism for small stations. A good example is Castle Howard, built in 1845 and now a private house.

◀ In the 1920s a simplified classical style became popular with image-conscious railway companies because it gave a sense of modernity and elegance. For the same reason, the style appealed to architects of post offices and government buildings. This is the new station at Clacton-on-Sea, completed in 1929 by the LNER, a company keen on the classical neo-Georgian style.

With no traditions to follow and well away from the big-city style wars, the builders of rural railway stations were free to follow their own ideas and develop their own styles. Many country stations had to combine railway functions with the domestic needs of the stationmaster or staff. Architects and builders were influenced primarily by vernacular details, materials and cost. The result is a nationwide legacy of individual and often idiosyncratic local station buildings that range from the basic to the extraordinary, a wealth of cottage-style structures that express the diversity, imagination and practicality of the railway age. Some simply looked like cottages or small domestic houses that happened to have a railway purpose, while others were created specifically and distinctly as railway buildings. Since the closures of the 1960s many of the former have become purely domestic, losing in the process any tangible railway associations but becoming satisfactory small houses. Materials were often local, and decorative details, where the costs allowed them, could echo regional traditions. However basic, the staffed station was an outpost of the railway company it served, and its appeal to passengers was of fundamental importance. Small stations were therefore generally well maintained, with comfortable rooms, plenty of seating and fires in winter inside, while outside gardens and flowers enhanced the cottage feel.

▼ In April 1964 tank locomotive 1445 pulls its single carriage into Berkeley station, en route from Sharpness to Berkeley Road Junction, in Gloucestershire. A single passenger waits, emerging from the rather grand station, which is not unlike a lodge of a big country house.

▲ The Darlington & Barnard Castle Railway opened in 1857, serving a remote region, with stations that looked just like cottages. This is Gainford, in stone with barge-boarding, it has in fact been a cottage since its 1960s closure.

▼ More chalet than cottage, Charlbury, in Oxfordshire, is a relatively original Brunel wooden country station of 1853, characterized by the hipped roof and pronounced eaves. This famous example has retained most of its GWR features today.

▲ Photographed in the late 1960s, Hope station still has the look of a small timber cottage although its style is typical of the basic staffed station all over Britain. The chimneys and the windows add to its domestic look.

20th Century and Modern

In the early 20th century railway companies became increasingly image conscious and keen to dispel any hangovers from their Victorian past. This was the era of fast travel, named trains, Pullman comfort and modern marketing. Distinctive house styles and branding were part of this modernization process, all greatly accelerated by the formation of the Big Four in 1923. Of greater importance, however, was the major upgrading of stations and railway buildings. In the Edwardian period stations had begun to reflect the popularity of Arts & Crafts styles, particularly in the newly developing suburbs. In the 1920s a refined and simplified classicism became fashionable, but far more significant was the impact of modernism in the 1930s. All over the network concrete and geometry came together with dynamic effects as the Big Four competed in their determination to present a modern image. The GWR initiated an extensive rebuilding programme, to be seen at Cardiff, Paddington and elsewhere, but more extreme was the Southern and its architect J R Scott, who brought a distinctive Art Deco look to stations such as Bishopstone,

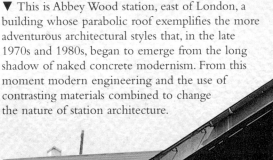

▲ In 1947, just before nationalization of the railways, the GWR published Next Station, their vision of the future. This included visionary designs for a number of stations, in styles that blended Art Deco with 1950s modernism. This classic design for Weymouth, with its great clock tower, would have brought the Victorian station up to date. It was never built.

▼ This is Abbey Wood station, east of London, a building whose parabolic roof exemplifies the more adventurous architectural styles that, in the late 1970s and 1980s, began to emerge from the long shadow of naked concrete modernism. From this moment modern engineering and the use of contrasting materials combined to change the nature of station architecture.

Surbiton and those along the line to Chessington South – places that reflected the modern image of the Southern Electric network. This was brought to an end by World War II, and by the time station rebuilding started again in the late 1950s, a new kind of modernism was emerging, with plenty of glass and metal used with brick or concrete, as seen in stations like Banbury, Harlow, Stafford, Chichester and Coventry. Some have not worn well, some are still memorable. The 1960s were characterized by concrete brutalism, but since the post-modernist, high-tech era of the 1970s and 1980s there has been a return to more sensitive, expressive architecture.

▼ The Arts & Crafts movement of the 1900s brought vernacular details, asymmetry and domestic comfort to houses. This influential and popular style soon imposed itself on railway stations. Bexhill, built by the South Eastern & Chatham Railway at about this time, is a typical example.

◄ Rebuilt in 1961 to the designs of N G Wikeley, Chichester is a good example of postwar modernism, with plenty of details that echo the Festival of Britain. Notable are the varied use of materials, the fascia lettering and the internal light fittings.

▶ In the late 1930s the architect J R Scott brought Art Deco, modernism and cinema-style geometry to the Southern Railway. This is Malden Manor, one of a group of four matching stations on the branch to Chessington South. Curving cast-concrete platform canopies match the dramatic style of the exterior. Rather surprisingly, these four stations survive, largely unchanged, as a memorial to the Southern's aspirations towards modernity.

SOUTHERN ENGLAND

Station Scenes

Southern England is one of the densest parts of the national railway map, criss-crossed with lines built primarily for commuter traffic. When the network was at its peak, there were also a number of main lines serving coastal resorts and harbours, along with a rich variety of rural routes and branch lines, many now lost. London sits at the region's heart, the routes radiating from its many termini. Dating back to the 1830s, these great stations, constantly enlarged and rebuilt, document through photographs the growth of railway traffic during the Victorian period. At the same time, other images and postcards indicate the changing patterns of railway travel – and reveal some of the forgotten corners.

▼ This Edwardian card shows passengers using Liverpool Street's original entrance, part of the 1875 station planned by Edward Wilson in French Gothic style. The station was expanded in 1894.

EXTERIOR OF LIVERPOOL STREET STATION, LONDON.

◄ Until its rebuilding in the early 1990s, London Liverpool Street was a vast station with a confusion of platforms linked by an overhead walkway. Here, in the 1920s, holiday crowds pack the concourse.

◄ Until 1924 London Victoria was two adjacent stations built by rival companies, and its grandiose architecture underlines that rivalry. This late 1930s, or possibly 1940s, view shows the eastern part, as rebuilt in 1908 for the London, Brighton & South Coast Railway. The Grosvenor Hotel of 1864 is to the right of the wonderfully uncluttered bus station.

▲ Euston, opened from 1837, was London's first mainline terminus and its most famous feature was Hardwick's great Doric arch, or propylaeum. To the nation's horror, this was destroyed in 1961, along with most of the original station. This card, posted in July 1908, gives a sense of what was lost by this act of vandalism.

▲ This 1905 card, extravagantly overwritten by a Frenchman to his friend in Strasbourg, shows original LB&SCR terminus of London Victoria, little more than a massive trainshed faced by a series of sheds and a porte cochère. This muddle, and the grand structure being created next door by the SECR, was the impetus for the 1908 rebuilding.

► After decades of chaos and muddle, Waterloo was completely rebuilt in 1922 as the elegant and spacious station in use today. One of its features was the massive concourse, seen here during the early 1960s. The fire brigade has arrived, but no one is paying much notice and the station's busy life goes on as normal.

◄ This 1930s photograph of Waterloo's original vehicle access to the platforms shows off the fine architectural detail of the 1922 rebuilding. Around the central window is a list of the counties served.

► At King's Cross in the 1970s a new travel centre was opened in the redeveloped concourse. This lady seems a bit lost in the old ticket area, having missed the signs to the new one.

◄ Equally evocative is this picture of a quiet corner at King's Cross, just before Christmas in 1958. There are piles of mail and luggage, but the station is almost deserted. Opened in 1852, the terminus was famous for its powerfully simple style.

▲ BR's public relations people were responsible for this evocative 1960 view of the ticket hall at Gunnersbury station. With the plethora of notices and an apparently abandoned bicycle, it is a scene full of period charm.

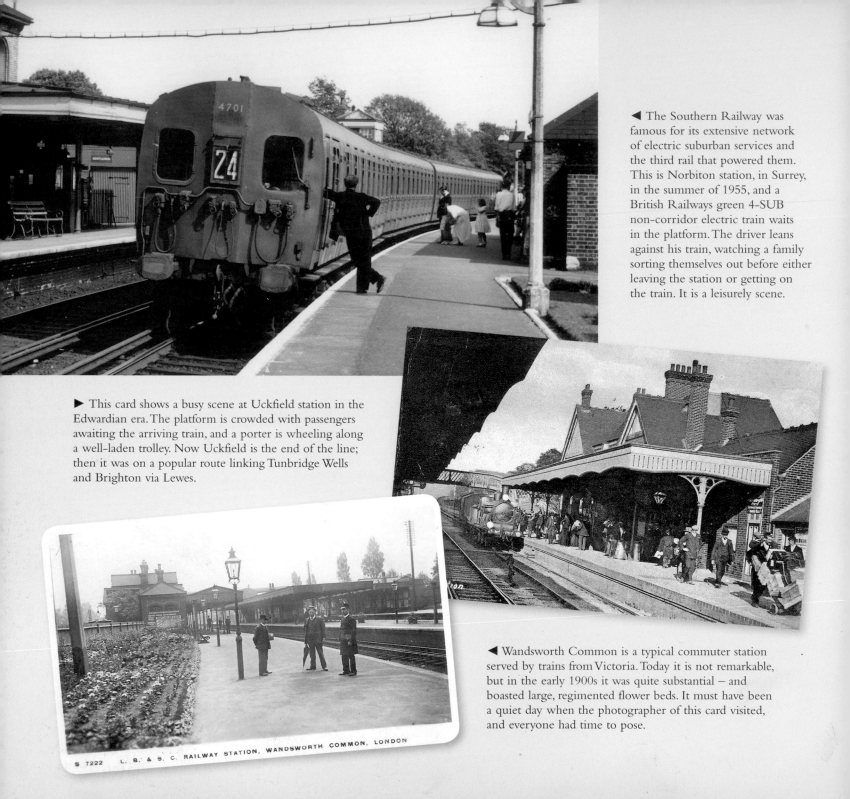

◀ The Southern Railway was famous for its extensive network of electric suburban services and the third rail that powered them. This is Norbiton station, in Surrey, in the summer of 1955, and a British Railways green 4-SUB non-corridor electric train waits in the platform. The driver leans against his train, watching a family sorting themselves out before either leaving the station or getting on the train. It is a leisurely scene.

▶ This card shows a busy scene at Uckfield station in the Edwardian era. The platform is crowded with passengers awaiting the arriving train, and a porter is wheeling along a well-laden trolley. Now Uckfield is the end of the line; then it was on a popular route linking Tunbridge Wells and Brighton via Lewes.

◀ Wandsworth Common is a typical commuter station served by trains from Victoria. Today it is not remarkable, but in the early 1900s it was quite substantial — and boasted large, regimented flower beds. It must have been a quiet day when the photographer of this card visited, and everyone had time to pose.

S 7222   L. B. & S. C. RAILWAY STATION, WANDSWORTH COMMON, LONDON

▶ The Isle of Wight's eccentric and idiosyncratic railway network was much loved, representing as it did the survival of a Victorian railway into the middle of the 20th century. This is Brading in the 1960s, shortly before the closure of most of the system. The station has seen better, and busier, days but services are still running and enthusiasts are keen to document the scene. The photographer has gone into forbidden territory beyond the platform to capture the scene while his friend notes the locomotive's number. Meanwhile a passenger, or perhaps another spotter, runs across the footbridge.

▼ This is Wroxhall, on the Isle of Wight, in September 1965. The train from Ryde to Ventnor drifts into the platform as the driver leans out to hand over the single-line token. Passengers, including a young mother who perhaps is introducing her child to the delights of trainspotting, watch from the opposite platform.

▲ Brighton has a classic seaside terminus station, set high above the town and still recognizably the building designed by David Mocatta and opened in 1841 by the London & Brighton Railway. In this 1950s view, the station concourse buzzes with everyday station life.

◄ Victorian railway companies were keen promoters of tourism, but many of their ambitious schemes came to nought. Typical was the short branch line serving Allhallows-on-Sea, on the north coast of the Isle of Grain. Allhallows never got going as a resort and few people used the railway, as this photograph shows. It closed in 1961.

◀ The Canterbury & Whitstable Railway was one of the first passenger-carrying lines in Britain, opening in 1830. This Edwardian view shows the level crossing at the start of the branch serving the harbour, originally opened in 1832 and closed in 1953. In a typically posed scene, everyone is looking at the camera: a lady with a pram, a young girl, and a gentleman doing his best to keep his balance on his bicycle while the picture is taken.

▶ In the first decades of the 20th century many railway companies experimented with railcars for use on little-used rural routes and branch lines. This 1920s photograph shows a petrol-engined and chain-driven example built for the Southern Railway by the Drewry Car Company. Seen here being tried out by senior company managers, it could carry 25 passengers and had a compartment for milk churns.

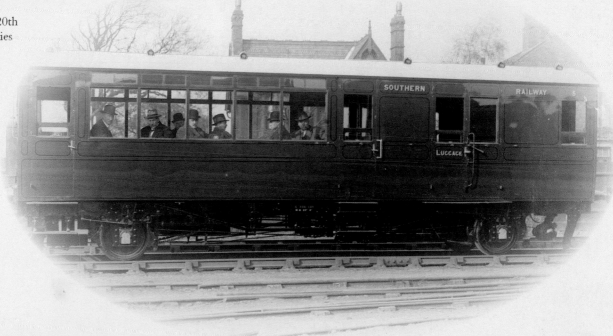

Brockenhurst to Lymington

hree railway stations today serve the Isle of Wight ferries: Portsmouth Harbour, Southampton and Lymington, of which the best-known and the busiest is Portsmouth Harbour. Least familiar to most people is Lymington where, as at Portsmouth Harbour, the trains are carried out on a pier over the water to meet the ferry boats.

The 4-mile line from Brockenhurst to Lymington was opened in May 1858 by the independent Lymington Railway, as a rival to the by then well-established route to the Isle of Wight via Portsmouth. At that point the railway did not extend beyond Lymington and passengers faced a long walk to the harbour. Not surprisingly, traffic did not live up to expectations, and Portsmouth, always busier and more convenient, remained the favourite departure point for the island. In 1878 the company sold out to its rival, the huge London & South Western Railway. Investment soon

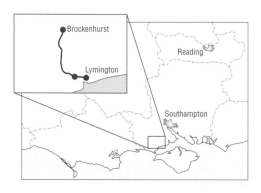

▼ In the 1950s, the paddle steamers were still in service. In an image full of period railway and maritime detail, the regular shuttle service from Brockenhurst approaches the Pier station, where the passengers will transfer to the steamer for a wintry crossing to the Isle of Wight.

followed, and the line was then extended to the harbour. The Pier station opened in 1884. Since then, the Lymington branch has continued to operate through the eras of the Southern Railway and British Railways. It survived the Beeching axe, was electrified in 1967 and is now in the care of South West Trains.

▶ For years the Lymington to Yarmouth service was operated by paddle steamers, one of which can be seen in the 1920s view of the Pier station, shonw here on the right. At this time Lymington harbour was still relatively empty and undeveloped.

(10 45) SOUTHERN RAILWAY. (787)

FROM WATERLOO TO

LYMINGTON TOWN

The route to the isle

For over a century the Lymington branch has offered passengers a relaxed and enjoyable route to the Isle of Wight, via Yarmouth, with the added bonus of an attractive journey through the New Forest to Brockenhurst. Although operated by relatively modern electric stock with no individuality, the route is still a good branch line experience.

At Brockenhurst passengers cross from the main line to the bay platform where the branch line shuttle waits. For a while the route of the branch runs parallel to the main line, then it swings away to the south to begin a journey across the open heathland and through the woods of the New Forest. The views are initially excellent, offering wide sweeping panoramas, and then the woods increase as the line follows the river to Lymington Town. Those not in a hurry will get out here to explore the attractions of Lymington and its harbour.

▶ In the mid-1990s a modern electric train waits at the Pier station, adjacent to the ferry. The view is modern, but the whole process of taking a train directly to a ship is delightfully Victorian and the atmosphere of Lymington Pier station has changed little over the years.

▼ In 1967, in the very last days of steam haulage on the branch, an ex-LMS Ivatt 2-6-2 tank locomotive pauses at the end of the pier. When the fireman has changed the points, the engine will run round its carriages to be ready to haul them back to Brockenhurst. This operation, which had to take place before every journey along the branch, is a reminder of the complexity of steam haulage, something often overlooked by modern enthusiasts who never knew the real thing. The setting, with views across the estuary towards the Isle of Wight, is magnificent.

The final stretch of the train ride, across the Lymington river on a raised causeway and on to the Pier station, is a classic maritime journey, a rare survivor from the Victorian period, when branch lines met steamers all over Britain. There are exciting views, and the harbour is busier than ever, filled with pleasure boats of all kinds moored close to the raised track. At the terminus, the Isle of Wight ferry waits, just a short walk away. It may no longer be a paddle steamer, but the atmosphere is still the same, as is the experience of the journey. This is usually best enjoyed on the deck of the ferry, as it weaves its way out of the harbour through the crowded moorings to begin its crossing of the Solent.

▼ Although primarily a passenger line, the Lymington branch did carry freight. In this Edwardian postcard of the harbour and pier line in LSWR days, a locomotive hauls a long train of fully loaded wagons back towards Lymington Town.

Lymington

Hastings to Ashford

In 1851 the South Eastern Railway, a company gradually expanding its network in east Kent, opened a line from Hastings to Ashford. For the South Eastern it was a logical connecting line, but for the residents of a remote part of Kent on the edge of the Romney Marshes, it was a revolution. Sleepy little towns such as Rye and Winchelsea, still stuck in the 18th century amid the mystique of the Cinque Ports, were suddenly part of the modern world. Rye was the main beneficiary, gaining a modernized harbour, a grand classical station in the Italianate style (William Tress at his best) and, ultimately, its own local railway network. Winchelsea was not so lucky as the railway kept well to the north of the town. Other stops along the route were at that time little more than wayside halts, serving tiny communities. In due course a branch was opened from Appledore to New Romney, Lydd and Dungeness, which traversed the flat marshland and made accessible southern England's most unusual and remote landscape. By this time Hastings was discovering a new life as a holiday centre and the old village of Ashford was turning itself into a thriving and rapidly expanding railway town to service the works established there in the 1840s. From this point not much changed. The South Eastern joined its rivals, subsequently becoming the Southern Railway and in the end part of the Southern Region of British Railways. The New Romney branch, which from the 1920s offered a connection with the Romney, Hythe & Dymchurch Railway, was closed to passengers in the 1960s, although part of the route remains open for trains serving the nuclear power station at Dungeness. Promoted as the smallest public railway in the world and deservedly famous, the Romney, Hythe & Dymchurch lives on in splendid isolation.

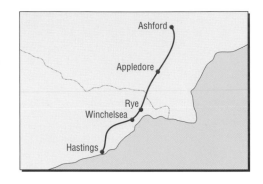

▼ 'Having a Good Time at Hastings' is the title of this photograph of a group of happy holidaymakers on the beach. It was taken in the 1930s, when Hastings was at its peak as a fashionable resort, thanks largely to the railway and its smart, modernist publicity.

◀ There have been several stations at Hastings. This early 20th-century postcard shows it during the era of the South Eastern & Chatham Railway, a smart and efficient company whose network covered much of Kent. The station then served many routes, to the west, the east and the north, and London expresses would stand next to locals for Ashford.

HASTINGS STATION-DEPARTURE PLATFORM.
SOUTH-EASTERN & CHATHAM RY.

▶ Although ignored by the railway, Winchelsea was a picturesque town rich in history and popular with visitors. As a result it generated plenty of postcards, which often blended rural romanticism with history. This card depicts Strand Gate, a legacy of the town's time as a busy port in the Middle Ages.

The Strand Gate, Winchelsea

From a Water Colour Drawing by W. H. Borrow.

The journey

Since privatization of the railways, the route between Hastings and Ashford has seen the comings and goings of a number of operators, along with their liveries. However, even in standard modern stock the journey is still a pleasure and offers, as it always has, a vision of a remote and little-known region of England. It is a true country railway, a kind of time warp between slices of the modern world. At one end is Hastings, a town built on history and a resort that has known better days. It is now graced with a new station, built to replace the former Art Deco palace that was a sad memorial of the town's great days in the 1930s. At the other end of the line is Ashford, with its glittering new international station, the gateway to Europe, surrounded by the clutter of the former railway works that were the birthplace of some of the most famous railway locomotives that ever ran on the railways of southern England.

▲ East of Hastings the line crosses the flat landscape that borders the Romney Marshes, framed to the north by a line of hills. Rye, set on a hill and topped by its church tower, is a distinctive and dominant feature, seen easily from an approaching train.

▶ The windmill on the river bank near the station has always been a distinctive Rye landmark. This 2003 photograph shows somewhat ancient Class 205 diesel-electric stock.

► Rye had two railways of its own, apart from the main line. One was a short branch to the harbour, but more extraordinary was the Rye & Camber Railway, opened initially to Camber Golf Club in 1895 and extended to Camber Sands in 1908. It was only a very basic operation, with primitive locomotives and a couple of ancient carriages, but its eccentricity added something to the town. It was closed in 1939.

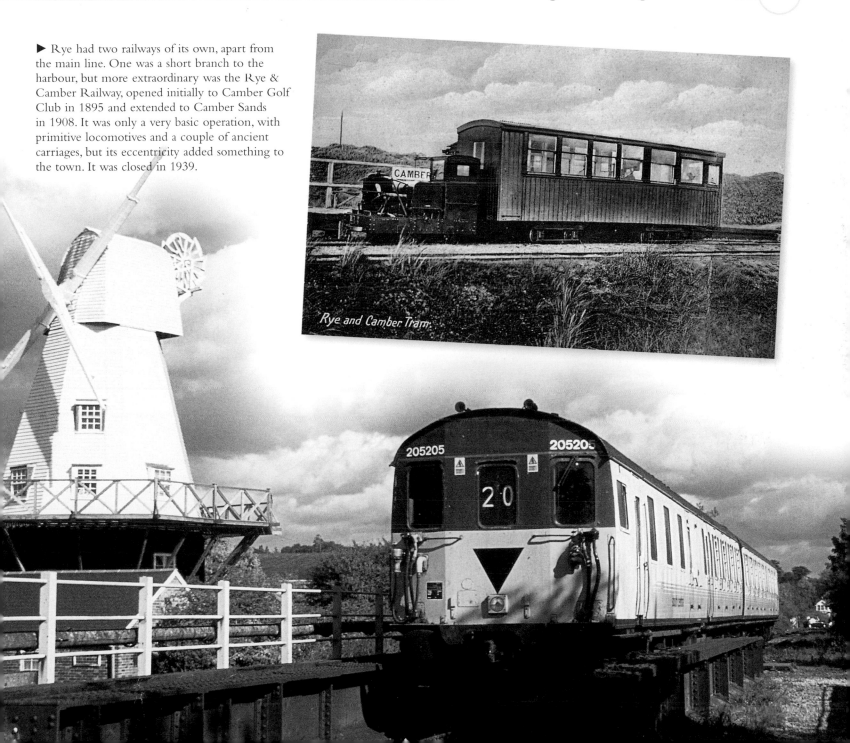

Rye and Camber Tram.

London Termini

Railways arrived piecemeal in the capital, responding to a widely felt but unspoken belief, particularly in government and landowning circles, that the new monster should be kept out of the centre of London. As a result the marauding hordes, in the the form of the new railway companies assaulting the city, built their terminus stations in a circle around the centre. The major attacks came initially from the north and the west, in the form of the London & Birmingham and the Great Western, although a couple of smaller companies, the London & Blackwall and the London & Greenwich, had also mounted early assaults from the east. A ring of 15 termini developed, ranging in date from the late 1830s to the late 1890s. They varied considerably in architectural style, as well as in size, reflecting the ambitions and wealth of a number of railway companies. Each was distinct and separate, underlining the competitive nature of the railway business, and attempts at terminus-sharing generally ended in acrimony and disarray. For similar reasons, most remained as termini, without connecting lines or lines that actually crossed London. Only recently, with Crossrail in the early stages of construction, are lines across the capital being built rather than discussed.

▶ When completed in 1866 to the designs of John Hawkshaw, Cannon Street was a magnificent station. Its hallmark towers and great iron roof survived extensive wartime bomb damage, as seen here in 1958, with West Country Class 'Whimple' about to depart. Today, only the towers remain.

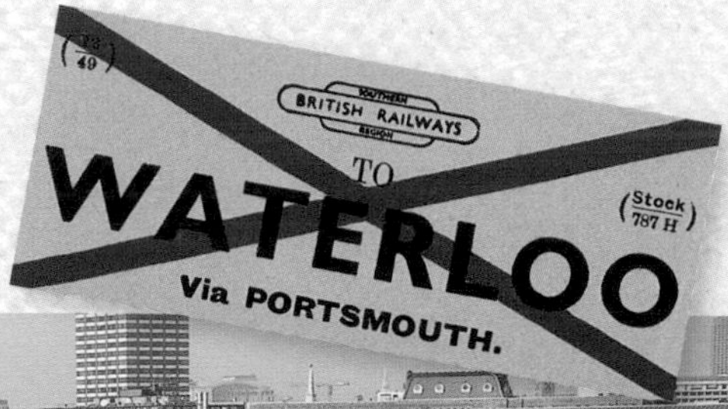

▶ Nicholas Grimshaw's international station at Waterloo was completed in 1993, its wonderful curve a great addition to the more rigid formality of the original building.

▼ This 1907 postcard shows the Hungerford bridge end of Charing Cross station. Opened in 1864, it reflected the ambitions of the South Eastern & Chatham Railway, which had been determined to have a terminus on the north bank of the Thames regardless of cost. Today, a 1991 building echoing its original shape rises over it, with the platforms squashed below.

▲ In the early 1960s British Railways issued Facts & Figures brochures about London termini, notable for their aerial photographs. This shows the 1906 roof of Charing Cross.

G. E. R.

St. Pancras

The first major terminus was Euston but others quickly followed, albeit not always in their final location. For example, the end of the line for the Great Eastern was for some time at Shoreditch, the Great Northern ended briefly at Maiden Lane while King's Cross was being built, and Nine Elms was a precursor to Waterloo. The major building periods were the 1850s and 1860s, decades that saw the emergence in their original form of Fenchurch Street, Paddington, St Pancras, King's Cross, Victoria, Waterloo, Charing Cross, Cannon Street, Broad Street and London Bridge. Later came Blackfriars, Liverpool Street and Holborn Viaduct. Last of all were Marylebone, arriving in 1899 and barely fulfilling the ambitions of its builder, the Great Central Railway, and Baker Street, turned into a terminus in the Edwardian era by the equally ambitious Metropolitan Railway.

The 20th century brought little that was new but much rebuilding. In the 1920s Victoria's two adjacent stations, run by rival companies, were united behind their splendid Edwardian façades. Waterloo, by tradition London's most chaotic station, was totally recreated with exciting, elegant architecture and the most efficient layout in London. Others, such as Paddington, were enlarged and modernized. Wartime bombing damaged many London stations, but only Cannon Street was never to recover fully.

▼ Peak Class diesel No. 45110 hauls a long Sheffield-bound train out of St Pancras in 1976, beside the famous gasometers. The new international station has totally changed this view of Barlow's great train shed, which for years was the widest span in the world.

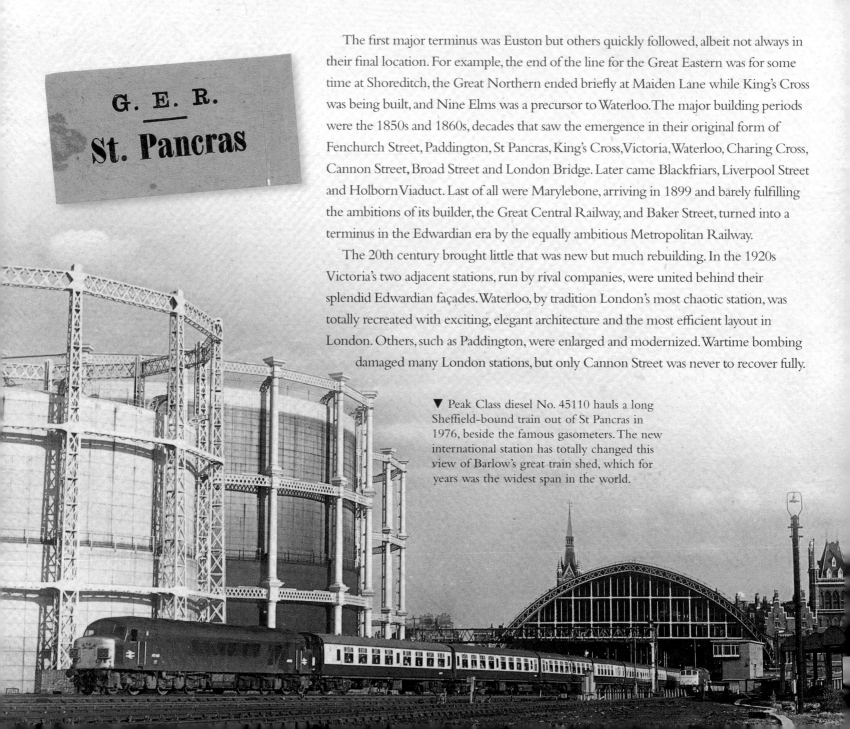

EXCURSIONS

FROM

EUSTON & ST. PANCRAS

FOR

SUNDAYS 5th 12th & 19th DEC. 1954

From EUSTON

Travel in Rail Comfort

BRITISH RAILWAYS

PLEASE RETAIN THIS PROGRAMME FOR REFERENCE

▲ Small boys, notebooks to hand, greet the arrival at Euston in the late 1950s of a Liverpool express, headed by Princess Royal Class 46207, 'Princess Arthur of Connaught'. Today, health and safety concerns have sent such scenes into history.

▶ Although perennially busy with thousands of trains on weekdays, London's termini were always keen to promote weekend traffic. This December 1954 leaflet advertised excursions to places as diverse as Derby, Dudley Port, Rugby, Tamworth, Kettering and Leicester.

Then, in the 1960s, came the wanton destruction of Euston station. One of the greatest architectural achievements of the railway age was replaced with a structure of total mediocrity, infamous worldwide for its lack of style and utter disregard of passenger comfort. Luckily the outcry saved the other great Victorian termini, and changes in the 1980s were more sympathetic. Broad Street, the least-used of all London termini, disappeared but in the process its neighbour Liverpool Street, another famously chaotic station, was magnificently restored. Holborn Viaduct and Blackfriars ceased to operate as termini, but Fenchurch Street and Charing Cross were changed in dramatic fashion when new buildings were erected on top of them, in New York style. This also happened at Cannon Street, but without the same architectural verve. In the 1990s the great hotel frontage to St Pancras, under threat of destruction for years, was finally saved and restored, and in 1993 London acquired its first major new terminus, the international Eurostar station at Waterloo, a remarkable building in its own right, brilliantly attached to but independent of the existing station.

Day Excursions to LONDON

12th SEPTEMBER 1962 to 3rd APRIL 1963 (except 26th, 27th, 28th and 29th December)

LONDON MIDLAND RAILWAY

◀ Broad Street was London's least-known terminus, yet its scale reflected the great ambitions of its creator, the North London Railway. By 1984, shortly before its demolition, it was little used by trains or passengers.

▲ A young trainspotter notes the imminent departure of A4 60015 'Quicksilver' from King's Cross in the late 1950s. Behind him an old tank locomotive is ready to take recently arrived Pullmans to the carriage sidings.

(37)
North British Railway.

King's Cross
(LONDON)

G. E. R.

From _____
TO

LIVERPOOL ST.
EXPRESS

G.W.R.

PADDINGTON

In 2007 the emphasis shifted to St Pancras International, with the redevelopment of the great station and the addition of a new international Eurostar terminal as exciting architecturally as the iconic building to which it is attached, itself reborn in fine style four years later.

Restoration projects have made many of London's termini look and work better than they have since the 1930s, but behind the modern developments, the cafés and the shops there is still that sense of achievement, history and quality that made them, in every sense, the cathedrals of their time. There is much to discover beneath the hurly-burly of daily use.

▲ On 22 August 1951 two immaculate and recently built Castle Class locomotives, 7024 'Powis Castle' and 7025 'Sudeley Castle', rest at Paddington, having just hauled the royal train into the station. The ubiquitous small boys are present but, even then, scooter riding on the platform was not encouraged!

SUNDAY EXCURSIONS

FROM

PADDINGTON

AND

EALING BROADWAY

DURING

MAY, 1955

Paddington Station, W.2.
March, 1955

BRITISH RAILWAYS

▼ Electric traction came to Paddington
for the first time in the late 1990s with the
opening of the dedicated Heathrow Express
service, operated by smart Class 332 units.

WALES

Station Scenes

The diversity of railways in Wales, built as they were by a number of companies, has always given them a particular appeal. In South Wales, the coal and valley lines made up one of the densest networks in the world, while elsewhere it was the demands of the landscape that made journeys memorable. Apart from the early route to Holyhead along the north coast, few main lines crossed Wales. Those that did followed exacting and remote routes. Wales as a whole was famous for its branch lines and country railways; most have been lost, but preservation has brought a few back to life. The photographs shown here have been chosen to reflect those distinctive qualities, particularly of country lines.

▼ In the autumn of 1959, at Letterston Junction, on the route from Fishguard to Clarbeston Road, the driver leans out from the train to drop the single-line token.

The Station Shrewsbury.

▲ There are a number of gateways to Wales, but the most important is Shrewsbury. From here lines built by different companies spread out in many directions. Standing on a bend in the river Severn, the remarkable 1849 Tudor-style station was designed by TM Penson and is seen here in an Edwardian postcard view.

▲ A man and his dog, and the fireman from the GWR tank locomotive resting at the head of a pick-up goods, pose for the camera on the empty platform at Presteigne in the 1960s.

▼ The busiest route into and out of Wales is via the Severn Tunnel. Completed in 1886, this great feat of engineering provided a direct route into Wales from Bristol. This shows Severn Tunnel Junction in 1964. Waiting in the platform is the scheduled car ferry service through the tunnel.

▲ The dense network north of Cardiff included a line westwards from Neath towards Nantgarw. In the 1960s, when this evocative photograph was taken of a pick-up goods passing the former Tongwynlais station, the line was near its end.

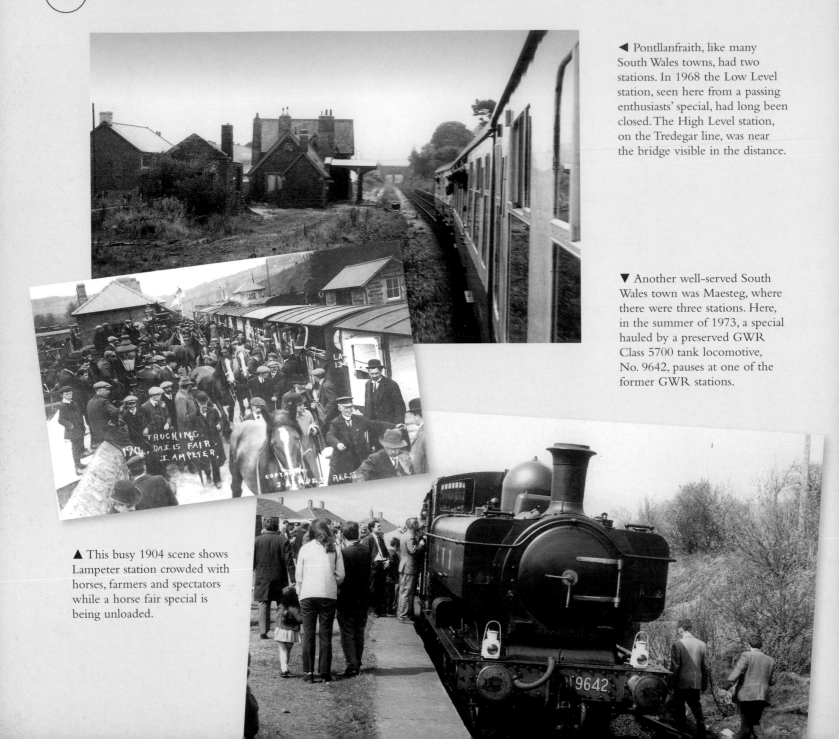

◄ Pontllanfraith, like many South Wales towns, had two stations. In 1968 the Low Level station, seen here from a passing enthusiasts' special, had long been closed. The High Level station, on the Tredegar line, was near the bridge visible in the distance.

▼ Another well-served South Wales town was Maesteg, where there were three stations. Here, in the summer of 1973, a special hauled by a preserved GWR Class 5700 tank locomotive, No. 9642, pauses at one of the former GWR stations.

▲ This busy 1904 scene shows Lampeter station crowded with horses, farmers and spectators while a horse fair special is being unloaded.

► One of the lost cross-country lines of Wales is the route from Barmouth to Ruabon via Bala Junction and Llangollen, closed in 1965. This is Dolgellau, or Dolgelly as it was in GWR days. A local autotrain rests in the platform, but most of the passengers seem to be waiting for something more substantial.

◄ Wnion Halt was a typically minor rural station a few miles east of Dolgellau on the Barmouth to Ruabon line. In the 1950s, two ladies continue to look out for their train as a locomotive running light passes through.

▼ The train pauses at Bryngwyn, formerly Bryngwyn Halt, on the Llanfyllin branch, and a passenger prepares to descend while the guard watches out for any late arrivals.

▶ This typical rural Wales scene shows a quiet day in the Edwardian era at Llanrhaeadr, south of Denbigh. The crossing gates are shut and there is plenty of time for everyone, including a mother holding her baby, to pose for the camera.

Railway Station, Llanrhaiadr, near Denbigh

▼ It is a sunny day in the 1950s and the local from Bala has arrived at Blaenau Ffestiniog's GWR station. A single passenger pulls on his gloves prior to picking up his suitcase, the crew of the GWR Class 5800 locomotive go for a break, and two station staff occupy themselves on the line.

▲ Llangollen station, set beside the fast-flowing waters of the Dee, is now the terminus of a thriving preserved line. When this photograph was taken in June 1962 it was still a through station on the line from Barmouth Junction to Ruabon. Passengers wait for a train, which the signal indicates is about to arrive, and box vans fill the small goods yard.

▶ In this photograph, taken in June 1975 from the same viewpoint as the one above, the line still looks remarkably intact although it had closed ten years earlier, in 1965. Track, signals and infrastructure have gone, and flowers flourish on platforms and trackbed, but the buildings remain. An enthusiast makes a careful exploration while his friend photographs the scene.

Llandudno to Blaenau Ffestiniog

As a centre of the slate industry, Blaenau Ffestiniog has a long railway history. First came the narrow gauge Ffestiniog Railway, whose 13-mile line opened in 1836 to transport slate to Porthmadog harbour. Passenger carrying started in 1865. Next came the Conwy & Llanwrst company's line south from Conwy, a laborious, expensive undertaking that took nearly twenty years to complete, even with the backing of the mighty L&NWR. The following year the GWR's rival line from Bala in the south arrived, its 22 miles having taken ten years to build. So, by the early 1880s, Blaenau had three stations, all inspired by the slate trade.

▼ In 1966 steam was still to be found at Blaenau Ffestiniog. A pair of LMS 4MT tank engines await their duties against a typical background of slate spoil tips.

Ironically, by that time the slate industry was in terminal decline. The Ffestiniog closed in 1946, only to be progressively reopened as a preserved tourist line. The Bala line closed in 1961, although a short section was kept open until recently to service the nuclear power station at Trawsfynydd. The Conwy Valley line, as the route between Llandudno Junction and Blaenau Ffestiniog is known, survives primarily as a tourist route serving Betws-y-Coed and other parts of Snowdonia.

Today the Conwy Valley line is one of Britain's most exciting railway journeys. From Llandudno Junction it follows the sweeping curves of the river Conwy, climbing into the hills through a landscape that becomes more dramatic mile by mile. By the 1880s tourism in this part of Wales was developing fast, and the L&NWR encouraged this traffic by building a hotel at Betws-y-Coed. This is still an important stop for visitors and walkers. Beyond Betws-y-Coed the railway follows the steep and rocky valley of the Lledr, forcing its twisting route up through the hills.

▲ Blaenau Ffestiniog is a setting without equal in Britain, thanks to the slate spoil landscape. All around are relics of the slate industry and the complex infrastructure of railways that serviced it. Throughout the 19th century Welsh slate was exported worldwide.

This was the section that cost its builders dear, in both time and money, for the route required numerous tunnels and viaducts, most notably the seven-arched Lledr viaduct, or Cethyn's Bridge, built in a primitive, rocky style to match its surroundings. The twists and turns come ever sharper, and eventually the train plunges into the long tunnel beneath Moel Dyrnogydd. The noise reverberates from the rough-hewn walls and the passage through the tunnel seems interminable, giving a real sense of burrowing through solid rock. At last, daylight returns and the train emerges into the extraordinary landscape of Blaenau Ffestiniog, a town almost surrounded by broken grey hills, the mountainous piles of spoil from the once thriving slate industry whose remains are scattered all about.

The station is the end of the Conwy Valley line but, as it is now shared by the narrow gauge Ffestiniog Railway, it can be the start of another exciting journey, this time down to the sea at Porthmadog. Together, the lines offer a multi-faceted 19th-century railway experience, a route running from coast to coast through mountains that presented the kind of seemingly impossible challenge so appealing to Victorian railway builders.

▲ An old postcard shows the railway's scenic route along the Lledr valley. During this part of the journey the train crosses and re-crosses the fast-flowing river against a backdrop of towering mountains.

► This early postcard view of Blaenau Ffestiniog reveals the total dominance of the slate industry. The branch line emerges from the long tunnel beneath Moel Dyrnogydd, surrounded by mineral lines and sidings. Spoil tips, traversed by inclined planes and narrow gauge lines, merge into the distant mountains.

CRIB AU & FRIDD-Y-BWLCH, BLAENAU FESTINIOG.   211275

► The qualities of the landscape that the Conwy Valley line made accessible to tourists and walkers were actively promoted by the London & North Western Railway, desperate to claw back some of the money poured into the building of the line. A number of official L&NWR postcards show scenes around Betws-y-Coed, including this one of Swallow Falls, posted by a visitor in 1908.

▼ In 1998 a modern, single-coach Class 153 sprinter has emerged from the long tunnel on the approach to Blaenau Ffestiniog to reach the dramatic climax of a memorable journey.

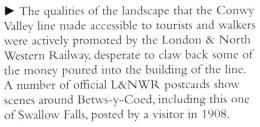

SWALLOW FALLS, BETTWS-Y-COED.
L. & N.W. RAILWAY.

Machynlleth to Pwllheli

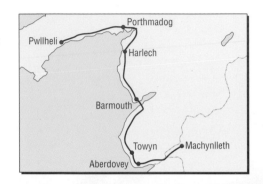

ainline railways came comparatively late to north-west Wales, with promoters and investors perhaps discouraged by the difficult terrain, the lack of significant industry and the small population. In mid-Victorian Britain, tourism was still in its infancy and the pleasures of the Cambrian coast were still to be discovered. Things began to change in the 1860s, firstly with the opening in January 1863 of the Newtown & Machynlleth Railway, whose 22-mile line made the west coast of Wales accessible to Newtown, Welshpool, Oswestry and Shrewsbury. The route included the famous Talerddig cutting, for some time the deepest in the world. Meanwhile, further south, the Aberystwyth & Welsh Coast Railway had gained approval for a line northwards along the coast to Pwllheli, via Barmouth and Porthmadog. This was planned to connect with the Newtown line at Machynlleth. It was built in stages, with the section from Machynlleth south to Borth and Aberystwyth opening first. By the time it was finally completed in 1867 it, and most of its connecting lines, had been taken over by the Cambrian Railway. This company, after a shaky start, was well

▼ On a hot day in the 1950s a locomotive simmers quietly at Dovey Junction, awaiting its next duty. The station is deserted, barrows are neatly parked and the signals are down – a common scenario at a station that came to life only when trains arrived.

established by the 1880s, at which point tourist traffic was rapidly expanding. This kept it in business until it was absorbed into the GWR in the early 1920s.

The period from the 1920s to the 1950s represented the heyday of the line, thanks to the rapid expansion of the holiday trade. The beaches, landscape and history of west Wales were widely promoted, notably by the GWR itself, and a named train, the Cambrian Coast Express, began to serve the region. Hotels and holiday camps flourished. At the same time the line carried plenty of freight, including coal traffic from south Wales, thanks to its connections with lines to north Wales and to the Midlands and north of England via Shrewsbury and Chester.

▲ Near Aberdovey the railway runs at the water's edge on an embankment overshadowed by great mountains. In this splendid setting a double-headed special makes its way along the shore, filled with passengers eagerly awaiting their day on the Talyllyn Railway.

From the 1960s the line declined rapidly as the freight traffic disappeared and the holidaymakers abandoned the Cambrian coast.

For a while, the section from Machynlleth north to Pwllheli was threatened with closure, particularly after the loss of nearly all the connecting lines, most notably the routes north to Caernarfon and Bangor and eastwards from Barmouth to Ruabon. In the south, the end of Aberystwyth's link to Carmarthen and Swansea made the Cambrian coast seem even more isolated. However, the line survived the Beeching era and in the 1980s was even improved by investment. This included the rebuilding of Barmouth bridge.

The journey

Today the Cambrian Coast line offers a delightful journey, with a route that passes through a varied landscape, never far from the sea. There are glorious beaches and splendid castles to be seen, and connections with steam narrow-gauge railways.

The train for Pwllheli starts from Machynlleth where the gabled station, fully restored in the 1990s, offers passengers the pleasures of plenty of original detail. Adjacent is a small stone building, the station used by the narrow-gauge Corris Railway, a former slate tramway that carried passengers between 1880 and 1931. It was closed completely in 1948 after flooding damaged some of the trackbed. There is a museum in the old station and a short length of track has been relaid. After Machynlleth the Cambrian coast line follows the river Dovey to Dovey Junction, the connecting point for the line south to Aberystwyth. After the junction the line crosses the river and then runs right beside the sea to Aberdovey, a quiet and old-fashioned holiday resort and in the 19th century one of

▼ In evening light, Barmouth viaduct stretches away across the estuary. Opened in 1867, it is the longest wooden railway viaduct in Britain. The steel spans at the Barmouth end used to open to allow the passage of ships.

NORTH WALES
THE MAGIC HOLIDAYLAND
REQUESTS
THE PLEASURE OF YOUR COMPANY
FOR YOUR 1961 HOLIDAYS

★ BEAUTIFUL BEACHES
★ LOVELY LAKES and RIVERS
★ MAGNIFICENT MOUNTAINS
★ ENCHANTING SCENERY
★ ENTERTAINMENTS OF ALL KINDS
AND A HOST OF
★ FASCINATING EXCURSIONS BY
ROAD, RAIL and SEA

TRAVEL by TRAIN to the NORTH WALES
HOLIDAY PLAYGROUND

LONDON MIDLAND

the busiest ports in Wales. At Towyn, whose church contains the earliest-known example of Welsh writing, there is a connection with the narrow-gauge Talyllyn Railway, a former slate line opened in 1866. Since 1951 it has been owned and operated as a tourist railway by a preservation society, the first line in the world to be saved in this manner. In the 19th century, Towyn harbour was filled with ships loading slate for destinations in Britain and around the world, but today little remains to hint at this once vital trade.

From here the train carves its way through rocky cuttings and then there is a fine view of Fairbourne's sandy beach and Barmouth Bay beyond. At Barmouth Junction, now Morfa Mawddach, the remains of the line eastwards to Bala, Llangollen and Ruabon can be seen. The section to Dolgellau, alongside the river Mawddach, is a footpath and cycleway.

The approach to Barmouth is magnificent, with the train slowly crossing the long viaduct over the Mawddach estuary. Completed in 1867, this, at 800 yards, is the longest wooden railway viaduct in Britain, and the last survivor on this scale of a type once common. Steel spans at the Barmouth end include one that used to open to allow ships to pass. The viaduct also carries a footpath.

After Barmouth the line runs slightly inland to Harlech, where the station sits far below the castle and town centre. Continuing on its inland route, the train passes through a series of small stations, Tygwyn, Talsarnau and Llandecwyn, with distant views across the estuary of the Dwyryd towards Portmeirion. Another wooden viaduct takes the train across the Dwyryd and then it curves round to Minffordd, where passengers can change for the narrow-gauge Ffestiniog Railway. This is the nearest station to Portmeirion,

▼ The appeal of Barmouth is timeless: its magnificent setting was as exciting to Victorian and Edwardian travellers, seeing the Welsh coastline for the first time, as it is now. This 1920s postcard underlines this. On the right is the railway, entering the town, after the dramatic crossing of the estuary on the longest wooden viaduct in Britain.

BARMOUTH QUAY FROM ISLAND.   A 298

Halts

The most basic, and in some ways the most appealing, type of station is the rural halt. These take the railways back to their infancy, when stations were just places where the trains stopped, places that lacked any facilities or amenities including even platforms. However, the halt is actually a later development, reflecting the increasing pressure on railway companies after World War I to compete with bus and tram services. There were, of course, always rather minimal or basic stations in remote regions, but the unstaffed halt is primarily a particular type, born out of this new kind of competition.

The appeal of the halt is its diversity, with seemingly endless varieties of both buildings and platforms. Halts were designed to be cheap to build and cheap to maintain, often consisting of little more than a rudimentary shelter, usually made of wood, and a single platform that was not infrequently well below than the doors of the train. There would be a name board, possibly a place for timetables and posters, and occasionally some form of lighting.

▼ Ivatt No. 41291 draws its single carriage away from Combpyne en route for Axminster, in Devon. This most basic station, seen here in 1965, at the end of its life, actually had a station building away to the left of the photograph. For many years a camping coach inhabited the siding.

▼ Two young women, perhaps going shopping in Aberystwyth, wait at Caradog Falls Halt as Manor Class No. 7826 drifts in with a train from Carmarthen on 11 July 1964. With closure looming, the station is looking rather unkempt, though the GWR colours survive.

▲ A smart lady going shopping and a guard starting his shift watch the approaching train at Blaisdon Halt in south Gloucestershire on 20 November 1963. An old corrugated iron shelter and a rather ramshackle lighting system suggest decay, but new concrete sleepers have been laid.

▲ The classic GWR pagoda station shelter is shown to perfection in this 1950s view of Nanstallon Halt, on the Cornish line between Wadebridge and Bodmin. This picture also shows a typical prefabricated concrete platform and name board, some smart lighting and a large garden roller, presumably for keeping the platform surface in order.

The shelters tended to look like garden sheds and were often scratch-built. Make do and mend, and minimum expenditure, were the guiding principles.

Some halts were built to serve military establishments, hospitals and other similar institutions; others were for use by workmen, and yet others were privately owned. Many operated on a request-only basis.

Halts are primarily in rural locations but there have always been some in towns and cities. These tended to be minor or subsidiary stations that saw only light or occasional traffic.

There used to be hundreds of halts all over Britain's many were lost during the closures of the 1960s, but there are still plenty to be enjoyed in the network.

Although the word halt has virtually disappeared from the modern timetables, traditions die hard, and on rural lines it is not unusual to hear guards on trains attaching the word halt to unstaffed stations when making their announcements.

CENTRAL ENGLAND

Station Scenes

The railway map of Central England has always been dense and complicated, made up as it is with main lines and big city stations, rural cross-country routes and branch lines. Some of Britain's first railways, such as the London & Birmingham, formed the backbone of this map, and then development continued into the 20th century with the completion of the Great Central and its network. Closures in the 1960s were extensive, affecting both major and minor routes throughout this large and varied region, which reaches from the Welsh borders to East Anglia in the east and northwards from London and the home counties to the Midlands. The legacy of this complex map is a great variety of platform scenes, from busy mainline stations to minor country halts, reflecting many aspects of railway life in the 20th century.

◄ The short branch from Kidlington, near Oxford, to Woodstock opened in 1890 and closed in 1954. This is a deserted Woodstock station shortly before its closure. The driver of the Class 5400 locomotive rests before taking the empty train back.

▼ A lady waves the train away on the little platform at Bradwell station, on the Newport Pagnell branch, while the driver watches for the guard's signal. It is 1964 and closure is imminent. Someone has written 'Marples Must Go' on the noticeboard. It was a vain hope.

▲ Brill, in Buckinghamshire, was the remote terminus of a branch that started life as an agricultural line in the 1870s. Taken over by the Metropolitan & Great Central in 1906, it became the most distant outpost of London's commuter network. Never busy, it closed in 1935.

► Another Oxfordshire branch, to Watlington, closed to passengers in 1957. On the last day of service, Chinnor station is packed with passengers and onlookers, including some boys who have left their game of cricket to have a look.

▲ The Midland Railway built a rural line from Harpenden to Hemel Hempstead. It had an uneventful life. Beaumont's Halt, seen here derelict but still with its nameboard, was an intermediate station.

► A busy scene at
Northampton Castle
station in August
1964, with a crowd
of enthusiasts waiting
for the departure of
LMS Jubilee Class No.
45654, 'Hood'. Castle
station served the line
northwards to Market
Harborough.

◄ Beneath a threatening sky,
a member of Olney's station
staff braves the rain on the
empty platform to watch a
locomotive and brake van pass
through. Olney was on the
rural route from Bedford to
Northampton and Towcester.

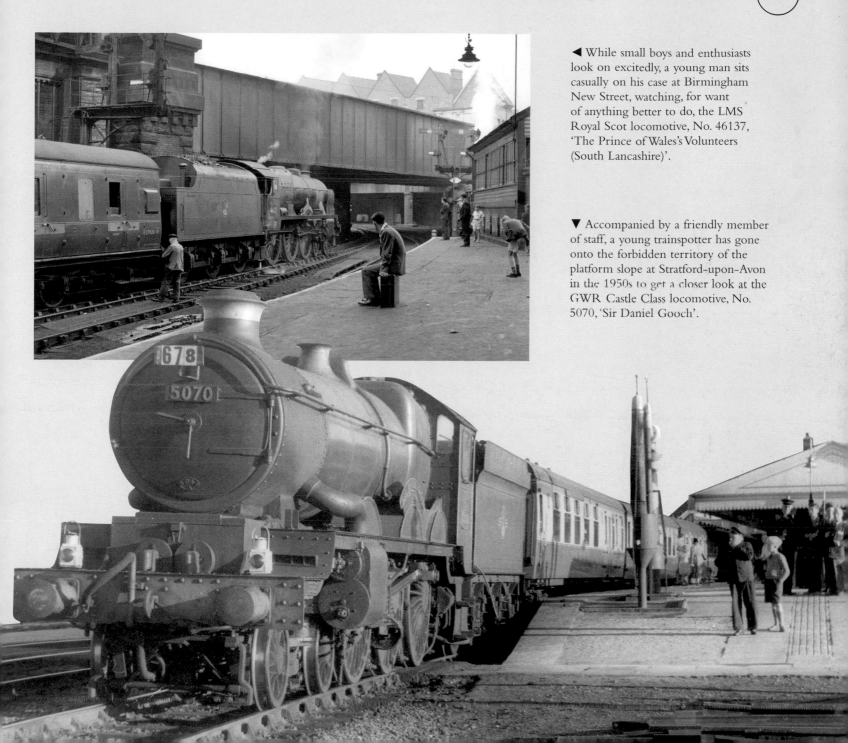

◀ While small boys and enthusiasts look on excitedly, a young man sits casually on his case at Birmingham New Street, watching, for want of anything better to do, the LMS Royal Scot locomotive, No. 46137, 'The Prince of Wales's Volunteers (South Lancashire)'.

▼ Accompanied by a friendly member of staff, a young trainspotter has gone onto the forbidden territory of the platform slope at Stratford-upon-Avon in the 1950s to get a closer look at the GWR Castle Class locomotive, No. 5070, 'Sir Daniel Gooch'.

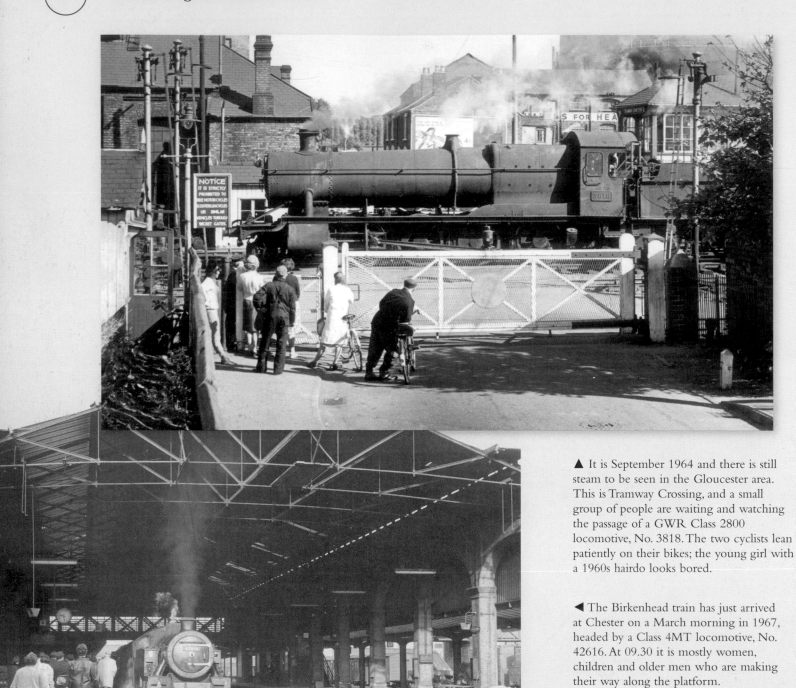

▲ It is September 1964 and there is still steam to be seen in the Gloucester area. This is Tramway Crossing, and a small group of people are waiting and watching the passage of a GWR Class 2800 locomotive, No. 3818. The two cyclists lean patiently on their bikes; the young girl with a 1960s hairdo looks bored.

◀ The Birkenhead train has just arrived at Chester on a March morning in 1967, headed by a Class 4MT locomotive, No. 42616. At 09.30 it is mostly women, children and older men who are making their way along the platform.

▲ On a May afternoon at Grantham, Lincolnshire, in 1975 just a few people are waiting for the King's Cross train, entering the station behind a Deltic diesel, No. 55011, 'The Royal Northumberland Fusiliers'. The man in the foreground with a dog, probably there to meet someone off this train from Newcastle, looks unimpressed. The locomotive was withdrawn in 1981 and scrapped.

▲ A small boy has a chat, in August 1958, with the driver of this Class 2MT locomotive, No. 41285, at Braunston London Road station, on the line from Weedon to Leamington Spa. A week later the line closed to passengers.

◀ In May 1959 an elderly passenger walks slowly away from Uppingham station, Rutland, while the locomotive rests between duties on this quiet branch line.

◀ Thrapston, in the heart of the Midlands stone country, was well served with two stations. This is Bridge Street, on the old LNWR line. It is a quiet day in May 1964, and soon the station will be closed, along with so many of the rural routes in this area.

▼ A shaft of sunlight, an old bench that has lost its iron nameplate, and an evocative display of carefully arranged period posters enliven the empty platform at Loughborough station in August 1946.

► Early morning on a sunny day in Nottingham Victoria in 1959, and a wheel-tapper and his colleague, seated on an old Great Central Railway bench on an otherwise deserted platform, are watching the departure of the 07.20 Leek-to-Cleethorpes train.

◄ Enthusiasts, male and female, explore the overgrown platform at Waterhouses station in Staffordshire in August 1958, while waiting for the return of their special train. Passenger services had ended in 1935.

► The station staff, together with their shunting horse, pose for the camera somewhere in the Midlands before World War I. Unusually, the stationmaster is well to the back, on the far platform.

Shrewsbury to Newport

The journey from Shrewsbury to Newport is a voyage through history, an exploration of the Marches, the borderlands that mark the boundary between England and Wales, disputed since the days of the Romans. It is, as a result, a route marked by great castles, or the remains of them, most notably at Shrewsbury, Ludlow and Newport. By the time the railways came, boundary disputes on a national scale were a thing of the past. Instead, there were many border towns, still slumbering in a pre-industrial age, that wanted to share in the prosperity of the early 19th century. Early railway schemes, therefore, had plenty of supporters and some industrial lines and tramways were being built in the 1820s. Plans for local lines followed, but the need for a major north–south route soon became apparent. In 1846 a 51-mile line from Shrewsbury to Hereford was authorized but work did not start until 1850. The first passengers were carried three years later, by which time the southern part of the route was also nearing completion. The builder of this was the Newport, Abergavenny & Hereford Railway, initially part of a much more ambitious scheme called the Welsh Midland Railway, which was never to be completed. By 1854 the whole route was open and it soon became the backbone of a network of lesser lines that connected with it or crossed it. At each end were major rail centres, Shrewsbury and Newport, and in between there were important junctions at Craven Arms, Leominster, Hereford, Abergavenny and Pontypool. It therefore became an important through route for both freight and passengers and a busy connecting line between south Wales and the Midlands. As such, much of it was used jointly by the GWR and the LNWR, although it was mostly in GWR territory. The pattern was maintained by the GWR and LMS after 1923. In the British Railways era, traffic steadily declined, and in the 1960s most branches and connecting lines went.

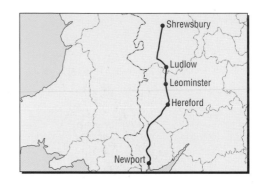

▼ Shrewsbury's great neo-Tudor station looks much the same today as it does in this early 20th-century view. Its style was determined by nearby medieval and 17th-century buildings, notably the castle and the old school. Completed in 1849, it was enlarged in 1855 by the same architect, T M Penson, and then again in 1903, without destroying its integrity. It stands in a loop of the Severn, at the centre of the town.

Shrewsbury Station

► Many of the stations on the route were minor halts serving tiny communities. All of these were closed from the 1960s. Typical was All Stretton Halt, just north of Church Stretton, seen here in 1957 with a stopping train from Shrewsbury to Hereford – a large GWR Hall class locomotive, three carriages and probably not many passengers.

▼ In the summer of 1988 a typical modern Marches line train on its way to Shrewsbury follows the winding route of the railway through a glorious Shropshire landscape. This is seen near Marshwood, to the north of Craven Arms and close to the former junction with a long-closed line to Wellington and the Severn valley.

Today, though still important as a direct link between south and north Wales and the Midlands, it is in effect a country railway with passenger services in the hands of diesel railcars. The only connections are at Craven Arms, the start of the Heart of Wales route, and Hereford, terminus for the line from London via Oxford and Worcester.

▼ A classic small town, and perennially popular with visitors since the arrival of the railway, Ludlow has featured on thousands of postcards over the last century. This is a typical Edwardian view, showing Dinham Bridge and the castle ruins.

The journey

The starting point is Shrewsbury's magnificent Tudor-style station, designed by T M Penson and completed in 1849 as a joint terminus for the Shrewsbury & Birmingham and Shrewsbury & Chester companies. Its decorative richness sets the tone for a journey notable for its architecture as well as its landscape.

▼ On a June Sunday in 1961, Hereford station is busy and steam is still king. A smart Castle class locomotive departs with its train, the lunchtime Shrewsbury to Cardiff service, while another, perhaps London-bound, awaits its turn. Hereford station is another decorative, 1850s Tudor-style building.

THE CASTLE & DINHAM BRIDGE LUDLOW

Highlights include Shrewsbury itself, whose castle is visible from the train as it crosses the river Severn; the gaunt summit of Caer Caradoc and its Roman fort nearby; the distant view of the Long Mynd; the wooded Onny valley; and, near Craven Arms, 13th-century Stokesay Castle, the classic medieval blend of domestic and military architecture. Another castle awaits the train at Ludlow, one of England's best small towns, set beside the Teme. Next is Leominster, a wool town with plenty of 18th-century buildings, and then the landscape becomes more open, scattered with the spires and towers of village churches. Hereford's cathedral can be seen, but not much else in that city as the station is well away from the centre. The line now enters Wales, with distant Black Mountain views to Abergavenny, a pleasant market town a long way from its station. From here, the railway follows the Usk valley south to Pontypool and the start of more industrial surroundings that stretch to Cwmbran. The rural landscape returns as the line curves past Roman Caerleon, and then it joins the main line from London and Bristol for the final entry into Newport. A handsome iron bridge carries the railway over the Usk right by the ruins of the medieval castle, an architectural conjunction that epitomizes the line.

▲ By 1965 services were already much reduced and diesel railcars were taking over, setting the pattern for the future. This is Llanfihangel, to the north of Abergavenny.

◀ In the late 1980s a class 50 diesel in Network SouthEast livery hauls its train across the Usk bridge prior to entering Newport station. To the left are the remains of the medieval castle.

Goods

For a century from the 1860s, freight revenues on Britain's railways were at least 30 per cent higher than passenger income. Indeed, many companies depended upon the carriage of freight for their survival. Goods trains were the backbone of the national network. Railways were vital for the transport of bulk commodities, notably coal, stone, clay, cement, bricks, oil, petrol and chemicals, and a whole range of materials relating to agriculture and food, including fruit and vegetables, milk, fish, livestock, grain and fertilizers, all usually transported in dedicated wagons. Equally important was the carriage and distribution of a huge range of domestic, commercial and industrial products, which included a national parcels service. For a century from the 1850s everybody relied on the railways to transport and deliver everything. Most stations had goods sidings and the visit of the local pick-up goods train was a regular event. All this was made possible by detailed record keeping and by a nationwide network of freight yards and marshalling centres. Today, after years of decline, only bulk cargoes and container traffic survive.

GREAT WESTERN RAILWAY. (999-1)

From _Gwestry_

TO _Weston Wharf_
_G W_

ROUTE VIA ———————— RAILWAY

Date _14/5_ 192_4_ Train _____
Wagon No. _94446_
Total No. Sheets

Consignee _R. E. Kirkpatrick Esq_
Contents _Sleepers_
500,000 W 34 Spl. 5/23 2.

◄ At various points in the network, huge marshalling yards organized the movement of wagons and their assembly into the right position, in the right train. This is Toton, near Nottingham, in 1947.

◄ The smooth running of the freight business required accurate labelling of every wagon to identify the destination, contents and client. In the pre-computer era these were prepared, recorded and attached to the wagon by hand. Every journey required a label, to ensure the wagon reached the correct destination.

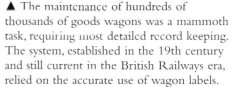

BRITISH RAILWAYS
— REGION

B.R. 11223

FOR REPAIRS

From ....
.... Yard

To ....
.... Yard

AT ....
.... Station

Date ....

.... Examiner

Any unauthorised person obscuring or
removing this Card will render himself
liable to Criminal Prosecution

▲ The maintenance of hundreds of thousands of goods wagons was a mammoth task, requiring most detailed record keeping. The system, established in the 19th century and still current in the British Railways era, relied on the accurate use of wagon labels.

▲ Until the 1960s the local pick-up goods train was a familiar sight and the constant movement of assorted railway wagons was the heart of the system. Typical is this mixed goods train photographed in 1950 on the Somerset & Dorset line near Cole, with milk tankers and parcel wagons under the control of an elderly 0-6-0 goods locomotive.

▶ The railways were early users of containers for simplifying the trans-shipment and delivery of a wide range of goods. In the 1950s there were thousands in use, and many of them could be interchanged between road and rail. Here a consignment of bicycles is being delivered from a specialized rail/road container.

Twyford to Henley-on-Thames

hen the branch line from Twyford to Henley was opened by the GWR on 1 June 1857, it was a short, single-tracked, broad gauge railway serving a couple of sleepy Thames-side villages. Things then began to change fairly rapidly, thanks very largely to the railway. With increased leisure and the popularity of boating, cycling and rambling, there was inevitably a considerable demand for outings to towns and villages in the Thames valley. Henley and Shiplake fitted the bill perfectly, and so the train service flourished. Henley had, of course, been known for its regatta since 1839,

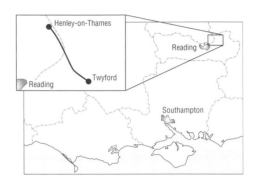

▼ In 1954 Shiplake was still a real station, complete with signal box, staff and a splendid lineside garden, seen here as a riot of summer colours. A young boy – perhaps he is a train enthusiast or perhaps he is waiting for a friend or relative – watches a grimy GWR pannier tank haul its short train into the platforms.

▶ Established in 1839 and given its royal status in 1851, Henley's regatta is now a major international event in the sporting calendar. In 1886, when this photograph was taken, it was relatively parochial but none the less attracted thousands of spectators.

▼ Henley's Royal regatta has long been both a social and a sporting occasion. In 1939 it was described as 'vivid with bright dresses and sunshades, a blaze of rich colour mirrored in the water and set off by the cool greens of the trees'. In the Edwardian era, as this postcard shows, dressing for Henley was already a social necessity for the crowds who came by special trains.

but the railway broadened the town's appeal and extended its season as a Thames-side resort. In addition, the opening of the railway encouraged commuting to London and so, in the latter part of the Victorian era, Henley grew from a small village to a substantial town. By 1898 the track, already relaid to the standard gauge, was doubled, the stations at Henley and Shiplake were enlarged and a new one was opened at Wargrave. An extension to Marlow was planned, but this idea was abandoned by the GWR because of strong objections from rowing clubs, concerned about the impact of this proposed extension on the famous regatta course. Matters remained the same through to the British Railways era. In the early 1960s there were over thirty-five weekday trains each way, with through services to and from London at peak times for the commuter traffic. However, this was a period of change for railways generally, and Henley was no exception.

Henley on Thames Railway Station, Arrival for Regatta,
H. Higgins, Publisher, Henley on Thames.

The 1960s saw the branch reverting to single-track operation and the ending of freight services. The goods yards were removed and, to satisfy the commuters, were replaced by car parks. Commuters also ensured that direct London services survived until 1977.

GREAT WESTERN RAILWAY

S.2

HENLEY-ON-THAMES

The holder is prohibited from entering the Company's Trains. Not Transferable
Admit ONE to PLATFORM   1D
Available ONE HOUR on DAY of ISSUE ONLY
This Ticket must be given up on leaving Platform
FOR CONDITIONS SEE BACK

7 | 8 | 9 | 10 | 11 | 12

1 | 2 | 3 | 4 | 5 | 6

2727

◀ Even in the 1950s Henley's grand late Victorian station saw plenty of traffic. The shuttle to and from Twyford, still a steam-operated service, was continuous, with several trains an hour. There were through trains to and from London at peak hours, and excursions during the season to this popular resort. At this point, there was still plenty of freight, and the station goods yards were busy.

A Thames-side journey

The journey is only a little over 4 miles, but it is still an enjoyable branch line experience.
Twyford has a typical 1880s GWR station, with the Henley services operating from
a bay platform. A sharp curve takes the train away from the station, and then the line
runs more or less due north. At Wargrave it meets the Thames and, soon after, crosses
the river by Shipley lock. From here the train is never far from the Thames and there
are plenty of riverside scenes to enjoy between Shiplake and Henley. Henley's station is
right beside the river, centrally placed for the town. Formerly a grand station with a train
shed and long platforms designed to handle excursion traffic, it has recently been rebuilt
on a smaller scale. It is now more in keeping with the simple shuttle service operated
by modern diesel railcars, successors to the famous streamlined railcars of the 1930s that
were developed by the GWR for
branch lines such as Henley.

▼ The Henley branch has seen many
types of branch line train. By the 1970s the
standard vehicle, as on so many branch and
rural lines, was the single-coach diesel railcar,
seen here on the sharp curve that leads into
Twyford station.

City Stations

The opening of the Liverpool & Manchester Railway in September 1830 was an important milestone in so many ways, not least because it was built to connect two major cities. At one end of the line was Manchester's Liverpool Road station, the first in the world, still relatively complete behind its impressive façade and preserved as a museum. At the other end was Crown Street, Liverpool's original passenger terminus, reached by rope haulage from Edge Hill, where locomotives were attached and detached. Crown Street has gone but the present Edge Hill station dates from 1836 and is therefore the oldest station in Britain still in use. Other intercity lines quickly followed in the 1830s and 1840s, for example the London & Birmingham, the Newcastle & Carlisle, the London & Southampton, the Great Western to Bristol, the Bristol & Exeter and the Edinburgh & Glasgow, all of which featured important city stations.

▼ The chaotic nature of Birmingham New Street is apparent in this 1920s view. Opened in 1854, New Street struggled for decades with expansion in a difficult site until it was, eventually, completely rebuilt by BR in 1967.

▲ The typical iron and glass train shed, seen here spanning the platforms at Birmingham Snow Hill in 1961, is one of the classic features of the city station. On a sunny day Western Region locomotive No. 7330 brings its long train to a gentle halt.

▶ One of England's best stations is York. Like Newcastle, it is built on a sharp curve, which in turn is echoed by the complex curving patterns of the iron and glass roof and the delicate flat-arched screens. York's first station was a terminus but this through station was completed in 1877. Nearly a century later, in 1971, it still looks dramatic and exciting as a train for King's Cross prepares to leave, hauled by a Class 47 diesel locomotive.

Indeed, railway companies were always ready to spend heavily on their city stations. The need to have sites near the city centres, and the constructional difficulties inevitably associated with such sites, meant costs were bound to be high. At the same time, a city station was for a new railway company a major statement of intent, designed to generate a sense of permanence and stability, bolstering public confidence and encouraging traffic.

PLEASE RETAIN THIS BILL FOR REFERENCE   N328/R/D

DAY TRIPS
TO
MANCHESTER
EVERY WEEKDAY
19th SEPTEMBER 1955 to 9th JUNE 1956
OR UNTIL FURTHER NOTICE

RETURN FARE   **6/9**   THIRD CLASS

LEEK depart 9.5 a.m.   MANCHESTER London Road arrive

Passengers return same day at
MONDAYS TO FRIDAYS
MANCHESTER London Road depart 5.17 pm   LEEK arrive 6.4
SATURDAYS
MANCHESTER Mayfield depart 5A22 pm   LEEK arrive 6.56 pm.
MANCHESTER London Road depart 7A45 pm   LEEK arrive 9.12 pm.
A—Change at Macclesfield Hibel Road.

FIRST CLASS TICKETS WILL BE ISSUED AT APPROXIMATELY 50% OVER ABOVE FARES

BOOK YOUR TICKETS IN ADVANCE
ACCOMMODATION MAY BE RESERVED FOR PARTIES WITHOUT EXTRA CHARGE
CHILDREN under three years of age, free; three years and under fourteen, half-fares.

NOTICE AS TO CONDITIONS
These tickets are issued subject to the British Transport Commission's published Regulations and Conditions
applicable to British Railways, exhibited at their stations or obtainable free of charge at Station Booking Offices.
For LUGGAGE ALLOWANCES also see these Regulations and Conditions.
Further information will be received on application to Stations, Official Railway Agents, or to Mr. A. L.
JOHNSON, District Commercial Manager, Trubes on Trams, Telephone: Stoke-on-Trent 8421, Extn. 36.

Travel in Rail Comfort

August 1955   BRITISH RAILWAYS   Archer Gaunt & Sons (Printers) Ltd.,
Heanor, Derbyshire.
BR 35000

(18)
Great Northern Railway
TO
Nottingham
(LONDON ROAD)

Architecture was very important, with the result that some of this first generation of city stations stand today as monuments to endeavour and achievement, for example Curzon Street in Birmingham or Temple Meads in Bristol. As the railway network expanded, more large towns and cities acquired significant railway stations whose adventurous architecture made the most of prime sites. By the same process, some cities acquired a number of stations, a reflection of the proliferation of railway companies. Indeed, there were in the end few towns or cities of stature in Great Britain that had only one station.

▲ As passengers idly await the London train, the sun shining through Stoke-on-Trent's ridge-and-furrow roof makes wonderful patterns on H A Hunt's Tudor-style curtain wall. The wall dates from 1848, along with the rest of this fine station and its matching hotel, but the roof is an 1893 rebuild.

▶ Influenced by Carlisle castle and law courts, Sir William Tite chose a Tudor style for the Citadel station, completed in 1850. This grey stone building carries the royal arms and the crests of the railways that commissioned it.

◀ Nottingham's station today is the former Midland station, a grand 1904 baroque and art nouveau extravagance. In May 1979 the St Pancras train, hauled by No. 45137, underlines the contrast between function and decoration.

MIDLAND & GREAT NORTHERN RAILWAYS
JOINT COMMITTEE.
Est. 1. 25,000. 10-29.   (18)

TO

NORWICH CITY

While there was no consistent architectural style, what many early city stations had in common was the enclosed train shed with a glazed roof spanning the platforms. Early examples in wood and wrought iron included Euston in 1837, which set a pattern that was widely followed. The classic arched train shed came with the use of cast iron, with which the span could be steadily increased. In 1854 the single span at Birmingham New Street reached 212ft, and others soon matched this. However, the crowning achievement in this field was William Barlow's great span at St Pancras, 243ft wide and 110ft high. The glazed train shed remained a characteristic of major stations through the 19th century and one of the last was completed at Hull in 1904. Nearly a century had to pass then before another classic glazed train shed was constructed, at Waterloo International, by Nicholas Grimshaw, one of the few architects able to match the inventiveness and daring of his Victorian predecessors.

▲ Norwich City station, at the end of the meandering M&GN network, was, in city terms, a notably minimal terminus. In this 1914 view not a soul is to be seen, just baskets.

▼ This May 1977 view of the Edinburgh train leaving Newcastle shows the operating complexity of the modern city station built on early Victorian foundations and the difficult legacy of piecemeal development.

► When it opened in 1840, Brunel's train shed at his Temple Meads terminus set a pattern for city stations. In 1964, a year before it closed, mailbags await attention and a child is shown the pleasures of steam.

Rapid expansion of city stations through the Victorian period often resulted in piecemeal development, which in turn led to operating difficulties and passenger confusion. Engineers struggled to find solutions by using different platform layouts and by trying to combine termini with through stations. Brunel, always idiosyncratic, favoured a long single platform serving trains in both directions, made workable by complicated crossovers. Most were soon swept away but a similar system survives at Cambridge. In many situations the answer lay in total redevelopment, but few companies had either the money or the inclination to grasp that particular nettle until things became completely impossible. The rebuilding of London Waterloo and Birmingham New Street are examples of drastic action forced by the threat of total chaos. In its architecture, engineering and operating diversity, the city station is one of the greatest legacies of the Victorian age. Most cities in Britain still have magnificent station

▼ Edinburgh's Waverley station fills a ravine at the heart of the city in a setting of architectural splendour, a glorious reminder of the power of the Victorian railway. Here, in 1971, with a Glasgow train departing, little has changed.

buildings, even if some are now no longer in railway use. It is important to remember that until the 1830s there were no such things as railway stations and there was no architectural precedent. Early experiments in London, Liverpool, Manchester, Birmingham and elsewhere were, seen with hindsight, remarkably successful in establishing a building type that could be developed all over Britain, and indeed the world.

▲ City stations have to cope with many types of passenger, all with different demands. Inevitably, suburban services are often shoved into distant platforms or, in this case at Glasgow Queen Street, into the basement.

EASTERN ENGLAND

Station Scenes

Eastern England's railway map developed steadily from the 1840s, when some of the main lines were built, often by predominantly local companies. A number of these came together in 1862 to form the Great Eastern. Local, cross-country and branch lines were added to the map through the last decades of the 19th century, notably the extensive and largely rural network spread across Norfolk by the Midland & Great Northern Joint Railway. In due course the LNER and then British Railways took over. In the 1960s many of the rural routes were lost as the emphasis switched to the main lines and the expanding commuter traffic. Much of the network and its infrastructure has disappeared, but there are plenty of photographs left that document station life in this part of England.

▼ British Railways was keen to underline its new and modern look during the early 1960s. One of several new stations built at this time was Barking, in Essex, seen here in a 1961 publicity photograph that highlights its predominantly concrete construction.

▲ The LNER used local exhibitions of locomotives and rolling stock to publicize its services and its modern image. Here, in Ilford, Essex, in June 1934, a gaggle of schoolboys wait to board the footplate of an industrial locomotive.

◀ Hadham, seen here in May 1957, was an intermediate station on the Buntingford branch, which had opened in 1863. The scene, as the driver waits to take the single-line token, is quite traditional, with an old bench and platform lights, but the nameboard shows that some modernization had taken place. The line closed in 1965.

◀ A busy 1960s scene at Abbey Wood, a Thames-side commuter line. The crossing gates are opening and a throng of passengers from the departing train push forward. On the other side, a Ford Anglia and a woman with a smart pram wait more patiently.

▶ A young, neatly dressed enthusiast poses for a friend on the platform at Beckton in the 1950s. Even then this was a remote East London location, the last passenger station on a line built primarily to serve the Beckton gas works – visible in the distance beyond the rather ramshackle timber station buildings.

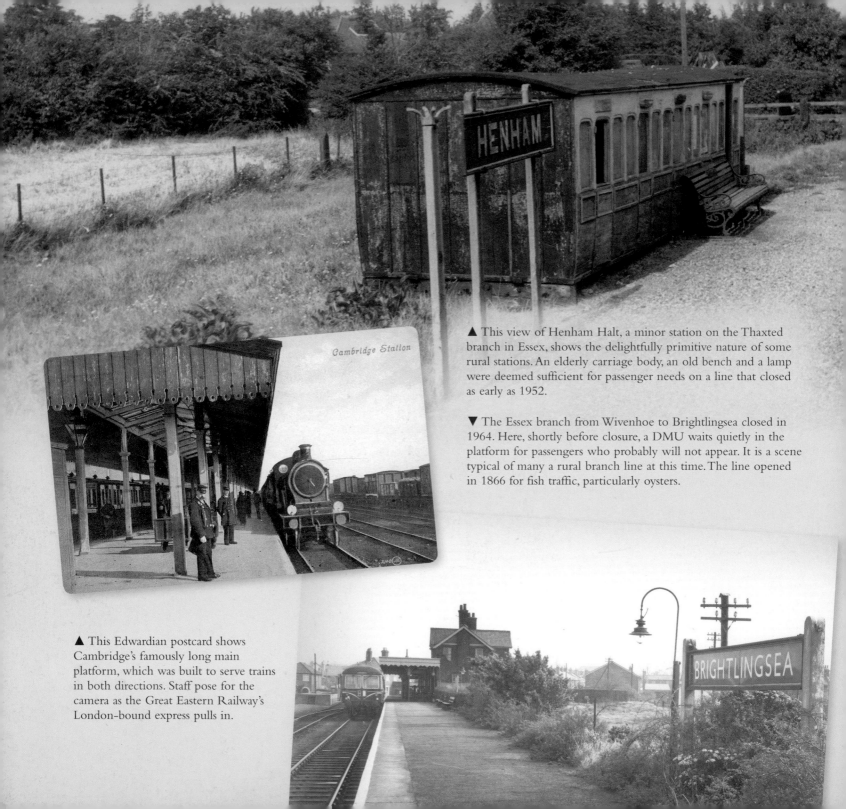

Cambridge Station

▲ This view of Henham Halt, a minor station on the Thaxted branch in Essex, shows the delightfully primitive nature of some rural stations. An elderly carriage body, an old bench and a lamp were deemed sufficient for passenger needs on a line that closed as early as 1952.

▼ The Essex branch from Wivenhoe to Brightlingsea closed in 1964. Here, shortly before closure, a DMU waits quietly in the platform for passengers who probably will not appear. It is a scene typical of many a rural branch line at this time. The line opened in 1866 for fish traffic, particularly oysters.

▲ This Edwardian postcard shows Cambridge's famously long main platform, which was built to serve trains in both directions. Staff pose for the camera as the Great Eastern Railway's London-bound express pulls in.

BRIGHTLINGSEA

▶ It is a busy morning in the mid-1950s at Dunmow, on the line from Bishop's Stortford to Braintree & Bocking, as passengers prepare to join an excursion to Clacton for a day at the seaside. This line, which had opened in 1869 after a long building period, lost its passenger service in 1952 and was then used only occasionally for excursions.

▼ As a railwayman cycles towards the station to take up his duties on a sunny day in March 1959, an express leaves Colchester, hauled by an LNER B1 Class locomotive, No. 61279.

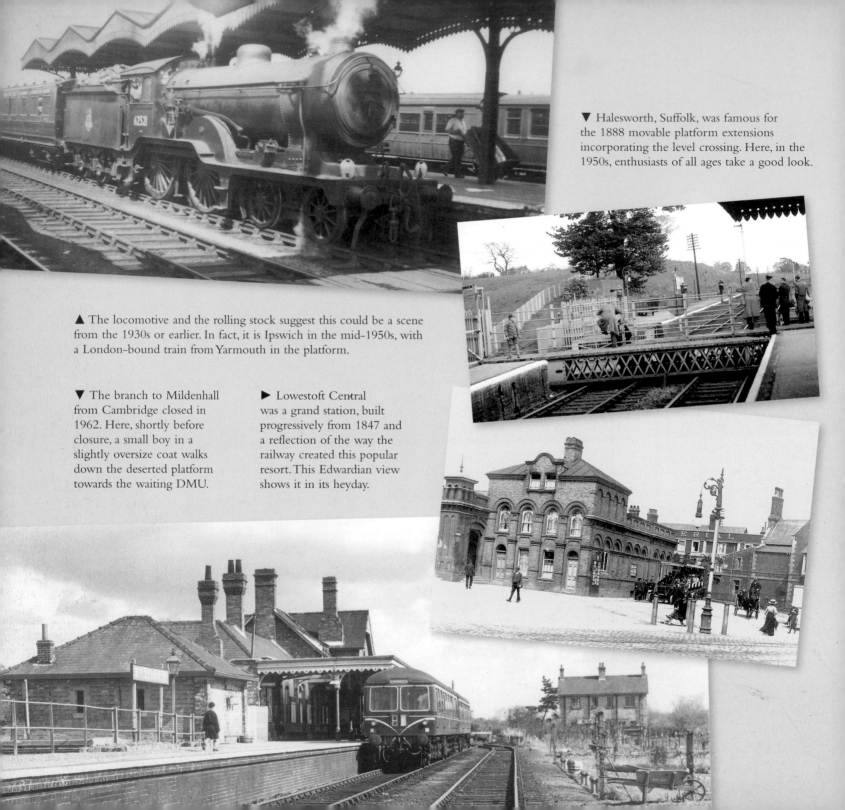

▼ Halesworth, Suffolk, was famous for the 1888 movable platform extensions incorporating the level crossing. Here, in the 1950s, enthusiasts of all ages take a good look.

▲ The locomotive and the rolling stock suggest this could be a scene from the 1930s or earlier. In fact, it is Ipswich in the mid-1950s, with a London-bound train from Yarmouth in the platform.

▼ The branch to Mildenhall from Cambridge closed in 1962. Here, shortly before closure, a small boy in a slightly oversize coat walks down the deserted platform towards the waiting DMU.

▶ Lowestoft Central was a grand station, built progressively from 1847 and a reflection of the way the railway created this popular resort. This Edwardian view shows it in its heyday.

◀ Wighton Halt, south of Wells-next-the-Sea in north Norfolk, was a typical rural station with nothing but a corrugated iron passenger shed, a lamp and an overgrown flower bed to its name. In June 1963 it was deserted except for a bicycle, which probably belonged to the photographer. The line closed the following year.

▶ Cromer High, opened in 1877, was the town's first station, but it was the better-placed Cromer Beach station, opened ten years later, that really made the town into a resort. Cromer High closed in 1954, and this shows the substantial station in a state of dereliction in 1964, shortly before demolition.

▼ Wisbech North, one of three stations with Wisbech in their name, was built as part of the Midland & Great Northern's network. After final closure in 1965, the buildings lingered on and were used for a while as a garage.

Marks Tey to Sudbury

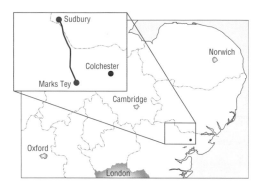

Some branches still in use today are in fact the truncated remains of former through routes, turned into branch lines by the closures of the Beeching era. A typical example is the 12-mile line from Marks Tey to Sudbury, now in many ways a classic branch line but originally part of an East Anglian network linking Colchester with Bury St Edmunds, Haverhill, Cambridge and Bishop's Stortford. The main line of this network was the Colchester, Stour Valley, Sudbury & Halstead Railway, authorized in two parts, in 1846 and 1847, and opened progressively from 1849. A link to Cambridge was completed in 1865.

These predominantly rural lines did much to open East Anglia up to both passenger and freight traffic in the mid-19th century. Construction was simplified by the relatively flat nature of the landscape, requiring few major engineering features but a very large number of level crossings. Each crossing was originally accompanied by a cottage for the crossing-keeper, and many of these are still to be seen, decades after the railways they guarded have vanished.

▼ In the 1950s elderly locomotives were still to be found at work all over Britain, but particularly on minor and rural lines. Here, at Marks Tey in 1958, two Great Eastern veterans, Class J15 goods locomotives, are hard at it, having lived through World War I, the LNER era and ten years of British Railways. Very few such antiques were to survive the next ten years.

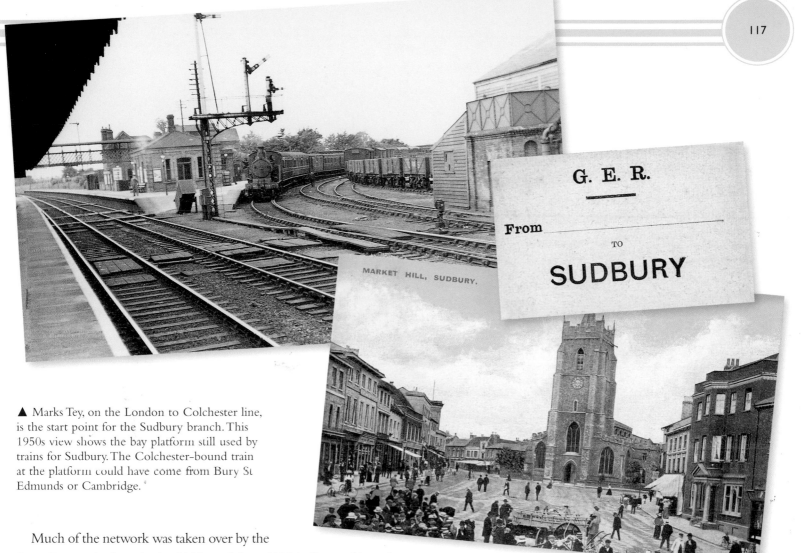

G. E. R.

From _____

TO

SUDBURY

MARKET HILL, SUDBURY.

▲ Marks Tey, on the London to Colchester line, is the start point for the Sudbury branch. This 1950s view shows the bay platform still used by trains for Sudbury. The Colchester-bound train at the platform could have come from Bury St Edmunds or Cambridge.

Much of the network was taken over by the Great Eastern Railway in the 1880s, and from 1923 it all passed into the control of the LNER. Increasingly under-used and under threat from the late 1950s, the line saw its first closures in 1962 but, for reasons that now seem unclear, the short section from Marks Tey to Sudbury was kept open. So, in effect, another branch line was added to the map. The survival of the branch has also facilitated the setting up of the East Anglian Railway Museum, at Chappel & Wakes Colne station, and the Colne Valley Railway, a preserved railway centred on the restored Castle Hedingham station on the old Chappel to Haverhill line.

▲ Sudbury is an ancient market town, famous for cloth and as Gainsborough's birthplace. At its heart is Market Hill, dominated by St Peter's Church, seen here in a 1908 postcard before it was ruined by cars. The message is intriguing: 'Rose & I are spending a few-days here. Are you not surprised?' A secret romance?

Constable country

The main attraction of the Sudbury branch is the landscape through which it passes, on the borders of Essex and Suffolk. This is the landscape of the Stour, whose blend of gentle hills and farmland broken by woods and river valleys is pure John Constable. Above it all are the huge East Anglian skies, bringing that particular sense of light and colour that defines Constable's paintings. On the right kind of day, the view from the train window offers delightful glimpses of Constable, and with it echoes of the East Anglian countryside of the pre-railway age. At the same time, it is a journey rich in railway sights, such as the well-preserved station and buildings at Chappel and the traditional level crossing, complete with cottage, at Bures. Constable died before the railway had made any significant impact on the landscape, but his frequent depictions of the locks and barges on the Stour navigation suggest an enthusiasm for the modern world. Had he lived another ten years he would probably have been impressed by the major feature of the Sudbury branch, the great viaduct at Chappel, whose thirty-two tall arches were built between 1847 and 1849 from over seven million bricks made at Bures. Engineering on this scale was unusual in East Anglia and has in any case mostly been lost. It is lucky, therefore, that the line still crosses this magnificent structure, exciting when seen from the train over 70ft above the ground, and spectacular when seen from the valley below. Peter Bruff was the engineer responsible, and he could not have asked for a better monument.

▼ Constable is the key word for the Sudbury branch. The railway, and with it the splendid Chappel viaduct, came after the death of the great East Anglian artist, but throughout the journey there are glimpses from the train window of the countryside that he loved and painted so extensively in the early years of the 19th century.

▲ In the autumn of 1996 a modern Class 153 railcar pauses at Bures. This type of vehicle is now universal to railways all over Britain, bringing to an end the regional characteristics that gave railways their appealing individuality. Only the liveries change, depending on which operating company holds the franchise. On this day no passengers get on or off, a common event on rural lines. At peak times, however, the Sudbury branch is busy, with commuters going to London and children going to school.

Ipswich to Lowestoft

The rural journey from Ipswich to Lowestoft is that delightful anachronism, a proper country railway. It is also a real rarity: an alternative route of the kind weeded out so assiduously by Dr Beeching. The quickest way to Lowestoft is a dash up the old Great Eastern main line to Norwich and then a local train to the coast. More leisurely, and far more enjoyable, is the country route via Woodbridge and Beccles. It is an irony that when it was built its investors, notably the tycoon and entrepreneur Sir Samuel Morton Peto, were inspired by the idea of a quicker and more direct route to Lowestoft that would naturally encourage rapid development of that town and its port. As so often, the line was built in several stages by different companies, and the history is confusing.

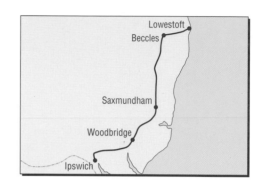

◄ Roses and decorative borders in the Art Nouveau style are commonly found on early postcards, often used to frame a range of images. Included with the historical sites of Ipswich on this card is a view of the docks, a major industry for the town and the railway in that period.

► There are two faces of Ipswich station, the mainline expresses to Norwich and London, and the little trains on cross-country routes. Typical of the latter is the single diesel railcar for Lowestoft, waiting to depart from platform 2 on a bright morning in 1994.

◀ Woodbridge is an attractive town set on the hillside above the tidal estuary of the Deben. The station overlooks the river and its boatyards. This view of the Crown Hotel hints at an earlier period in the town's history, before the railway arrived in the late 1850s.

First came the Halesworth, Beccles & Haddiscoe Railway, opened in 1854 to give inland towns access to Lowestoft and Norwich. Other small companies, the Yarmouth & Haddiscoe and the Lowestoft & Beccles, added bits and pieces. These and others were formed into the East Suffolk Railway from 1854, and it was this company that completed the line to Ipswich in 1859. A number of branches were also built, serving Framlingham, Snape and Aldeburgh. The line to Felixstowe, built by the Felixstowe Railway & Dock Company, came much later, in 1877, by which time the whole network had been merged into the Great Eastern Railway. The GER ran the East Suffolk line and its connections as a useful secondary route. Most traffic was, as a result, local and there were few through passenger services until after the 1920s, when holiday specials increased. Freight services were also mainly local, though the route was used by through milk and fish trains. Agriculture, local industry and the local harbours were the primary freight users.

▲ Saxmundham station is a typical east Suffolk station, square and classical in a simple manner. Today much of the route is single tracked and trains are rarely more than a couple of carriages. The long platform hints at greater things in the past, but this was always primarily a local line. Until the 1960s, passengers for Aldeburgh changed here.

▼ In a classic 1950s scene the Yarmouth South Town to Ipswich train pulls away from Woodbridge station, with the driver keeping a good lookout. Today this journey is impossible as the line northwards from Beccles to Yarmouth is long gone.

Things stayed the same until the 1960s, by which time freight traffic had virtually ended. The branches were pruned, except for the flourishing Felixstowe line, which now served the giant container port. The Aldeburgh branch was also kept open to Leiston, for the nuclear power station at Sizewell. Today little has changed. The line is well used by local people, for school, work and play, and the single- or two-car trains are often full. The timetable is if anything better than it was in the 19th century.

THE SOUTHWOLD EXPRESS — THE ENGINE JUMPS THE RAILS OWING TO EXCESSIVE SPEED, THE SKILL OF THE DRIVER ALONE SAVES ALL FROM INJURY.

The journey

The journey is one of quiet pleasures: gentle East Anglian landscapes under big skies, with echoes of paintings by Cotman and Constable; pleasant river valleys with views of woodland and old farms; classic country towns, Woodbridge, Saxmundham, Halesworth, Beccles, many with great churches and the unchanged atmosphere of rural England. All are worth leaving the train for, even if the stations themselves are not always alluring. Halesworth was also the connecting point for the eccentric Southwold Railway, whose 9-mile narrow-gauge line followed the pretty valley of the Blyth. Set up in the 1870s, it offered four trains a day each way, and passengers travelled at 16 miles per hour in Continental-style carriages with verandas at each end. Dependent on tourists with time on their hands, it never really recovered from World War I and it closed in 1929, by which time the journey could be made much more quickly by car or bus.

▲ The erratic and decidedly slow trains on the narrow-gauge Southwold Railway inspired a series of comic cards before the line's closure in 1929. Surprisingly, at its peak in the early 1900s, the railway carried over 100,000 passengers a year as well as a fair amount of freight.

After Beccles, once the meeting point for four lines, including a direct route to Yarmouth, the train swings east to follow the Waveney valley through a flat landscape dominated by the presence of the sea ahead and the changing quality of light. Caravans, as ever, are the harbingers of the seaside. At one time a line went due east to Lowestoft harbour, but now the train turns north and a swing bridge takes the line across Lake Lothing, the stretch of water linking Oulton Broad to the Waveney. This is now a landscape busy with yachts and cruisers in the summer and filled with maritime life all year. Bizarrely, Oulton Broad still has two stations, North and South, a short walk apart but on different lines, and thus inaccessible from the same train. Here the train joins the Norwich line for the final approach to Lowestoft, past the docks and acres of empty sidings and dereliction. Long holiday specials and lines of fish vans were the lifeblood of the place but everything has gone now and only echoes remain of this active past. As a result Lowestoft station, much reduced, is a sad place. At least it is central, as its original name implies, and the town centre and the sea are close at hand.

◀ Lowestoft now has only one station, and that is pretty basic. In 1994, although Lowestoft North was long gone, this old British Railways enamel sign in Eastern Region colours indicated that things had once been different. At that time such survivals were not uncommon.

▶ Nowadays Lowestoft is known for its docks and its fishing fleet, but this picture of the yacht basin is a reminder that in the early 20th century it was also a fashionable resort. Smart people, and smart yachts moored in neat rows, show us a different view of the town.

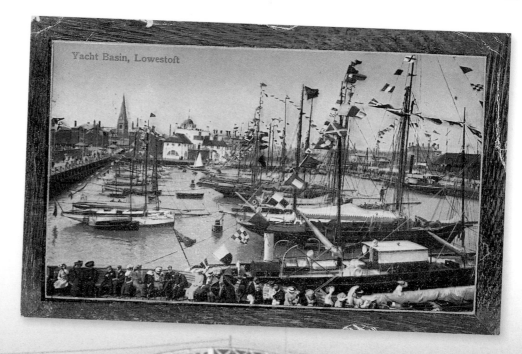

Yacht Basin, Lowestoft

▼ One of the main points of interest on the approach to Lowestoft is the swing bridge that connects the two sides of Oulton Broad. In 1958 a train from Ipswich with two carriages makes its way across.

Country Stations

The steady expansion of the railway network across Britain from the 1830s made accessible thousands of small towns and villages that hitherto had been remote and largely isolated. Railways offered mobility to millions of people via the thousands of local stations built to serve almost every corner of the British Isles. Thus was born the typical country station, the most characteristic creation of the railway age yet remarkably diverse in style and structure. A country station was almost infinitely variable in size but usually had one or two platforms, a waiting room and ticket office, lavatories and a lamp room. Some had a stationmaster's office and facilities for parcels and left luggage. These passenger facilities were often sited within a multi-purpose building that could also be the stationmaster's house.

▶ In the summer of 1971 two passengers wait for the train at Toller, a station on the branch line from Maiden Newton to Bridport, in Dorset. Never busy, the small wooden station that served an extensive rural community is looking sad and uncared for. It closed in 1974.

▼ Llanfyllin was at the end of a branch line from Llanymynech, near Welshpool. In 1961 seven trains ran each way on weekdays, but the end was near. In 1932, as can be seen here, the train was at the heart of village life.

▶A group of Edwardian children pose with the stationmaster at Cliddesden, a small station on the line between Basingstoke and Alton, in Hampshire. It closed to the public in 1932 but shot to stardom when it was used in the filming of the classic railway film *Oh, Mr Porter!* in 1937. Subsequently the line was dismantled and the rather basic, shed-like station was destroyed.

The platforms might be connected by a footbridge. In some cases there would be a number of associated structures, for example a signal box, a goods shed, a loading ramp, a water tower and, in country termini at the end of branch lines, a small engine shed. There could also be a network of sidings, to handle the goods traffic that kept the place alive.

The country station quickly became the heart of its community, a social centre for people travelling to and fro, and the point through which passed all supplies, materials and foodstuffs, all manufactured goods and agricultural produce. Newspapers and the mail came through the station and telegrams could be sent and received, making it a vital communications centre. Local shops were dependent on the railway, along with local businesses and farms. In its heyday the country station could and would handle everything, from livestock to bicycles, from building supplies to biscuits, from machinery to clothing and from coal to beer.

G.W.R.

Dursley

Mid. Rly.

(18) ¥ 20—10,000—5-10.   (W. & S. Ltd.)
Great Northern Railway.

TO

SPILSBY

▼ Leaning casually on his bicycle and framed by the extraordinary architecture of Dursley station, a young man, perhaps awaiting his girl, watches the train for Coaley Junction getting ready to depart in July 1947, headed by an elderly former Midland Railway tank locomotive.

▲ Long closed to passengers, Shipston-on-Stour was kept alive by occasional goods traffic until May 1960. Photographed in the summer of 1959, it looks in every sense like the end of the line.

▼ Spilsby, seen here in July 1954, was a quite substantial station at the end of a short Lincolnshire branch line. There are cattle and tank wagons in the sidings, the goods shed is full, but there are no passengers in sight.

Its buildings witnessed throughout the year the daily life of the people living in the town or village, young and old, in sickness and in health, and from its platforms children went to school, men and women went about their business or away on trips and visits, ladies went shopping and the young carried out their courting. The station staff were familiar figures in the local hierarchy with many living locally, and in a small community the stationmaster was a widely respected figure of considerable stature and importance.

▲ In this perfect country railway scene, a push-pull train with a GWR pannier tank waits to depart from Marsh Mills station, in south Devon. It is 1961 and mothers and their children, in light summer clothes, have returned from a shopping trip to Plymouth. The driver waits, and the signalman watches from his window, ready to send the train away as soon as the passengers have safely crossed the tracks.

Country stations were built in timber, brick or stone, their size and architectural complexity reflective of both the importance of the town or village and the wealth of the railway company that built them. Some single-storey buildings were little more than halts, while others were far more complex and significant, with plenty of decorative details often echoing vernacular styles and traditions. For about a century the country station thrived as an indispensable element in the social structure of rural Britain, enjoying as it did a monopoly in all the services it offered. However, competition from road transport became a major threat from the 1930s, initially from coaches and then increasingly from private cars. By the 1950s country railways, and thus country stations, were in serious decline, with many kept in business only by the goods and freight services they continued to offer. Facilities and staff were withdrawn and buildings were closed up or even demolished. When Dr Beeching published his report in 1963, he recommended the closure of over 2,000 stations, the majority of which were sited in small towns and villages. Some areas, notably rural Scotland and Wales, were particularly hard hit, losing not only local stations but entire routes.

▼Earls Colne was a typical country station on the rural East Anglian line from Haverhill to Chappel & Wakes Colne via Halstead. This carefully posed photograph, complete with the statutory children, shows the station in the Edwardian era. Judging by the photographer's position, and knowing the time it must have taken to set up the shot, trains were clearly not very frequent.

G. E. R.

From _____

TO

EARLS COLNE

Goudhurst

Hundreds of country stations were lost, along with their history and their long tradition of community service. The majority were demolished but there were many that survived, sold off and converted to domestic or business use. These can usually be readily identified and are often well cared-for, at the centre of rural communities increasingly devastated by the spread of road transport. It is an irony that the solution to the problem faced by so many small towns and villages could have been the country railway.

◄ Rural East Anglia was particularly well served by railways, the Victorians having built an extensive network that brought life to so many isolated communities. Typical was the line that went south from Swaffham through empty farmland to Roundham Junction and Thetford. Stow Bedon was one of the little villages on the line, yet the station, in local flint and brick, was comparatively substantial. Here, on a quiet, clear winter's day in the 1950s, two women and a child walk away from the platform. This line closed in 1964, along with many other East Anglian routes.

▼ Striking stone architecture, complete with stepped gables, a pretty canopy, a tidy little signal box and spectacular scenery, makes Dalmally a country station worth visiting. It is on the line from Crianlarich to Oban, to the east of Loch Awe. Handsome stations serving small communities are a feature of many of Scotland's rural routes.

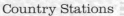

◀ The Hawkhurst branch, in Kent, was notable for its very tall station buildings, far larger than the line would seem to justify. This is Goudhurst, on a quiet day in the early 1960s. A train waits to depart, a passenger wanders past, but otherwise the place seems to be deserted. A motorcycle is parked on the platform – perhaps the signalman has left it there, ready for the end of his shift.

▼ Bishops Waltham, seen here on a quiet day in 1959, was an extravagantly grand station at the end of a minor Hampshire branch line. The scale and richness of the architectural decoration seems out of place.

NORTHERN ENGLAND

Station Scenes

The North of England has long been blessed by a remarkable range of stations, from big city termini to remote country halts. It was here that the railways were invented and developed, so the habit of going to stations and taking, or watching, trains was instilled early in the minds of a curious public. As elsewhere, the images selected indicate the endless diversity of the photographer's imagination and vision. Some photographers like crowded scenes, some emptiness, some pick the special occasion, and some give the impression that they just happened to be passing. What unites them is their love of railways, and their legacy is a mixture of the familiar and the unfamiliar, the scenes still to be enjoyed and those lost for ever.

42

CENTRAL STATION, MANCHESTER.

▲ Manchester Central is lost as a city terminus, though the main building survives as an exhibition centre. It seems unusually quiet in this postcard view, but its importance early in the 20th century is clear.

◀ A rare moment, captured on 1 July 1983, when British Rail's experimental Advanced Passenger Train made a visit to Manchester Piccadilly: the train is ready to leave the almost empty platform, and the guard is a blur of activity.

▼ The British Railways photographer must have waited a long time at Carlisle to pick a moment, probably in the 1960s, when nothing was happening and the platforms were largely deserted, at 11.18.

▲ Southport Chapel Street was, in 1958, one of at least seven stations either serving the town or having 'Southport' incorporated in its name. Prior to the departure of the 09.55 to Manchester on a cold December morning, stationmaster and driver confer – once a common event to be witnessed at big stations everywhere.

◄ It is a summer's day at York in 1973 and there are plenty of people awaiting the London train. In the foreground a girl with fashionable wedge heels checks her luggage. Over on the opposite platform the Cardiff train is about to depart.

► Like Southport, Blackpool was well
served by stations. It was, after all, a resort
largely created by the railway and when this
photograph was taken in 1925 it was entirely
dependent on the railway for its holiday traffic.
This is the concourse at Blackpool Talbot
Road, or North as it became, and it is a scene
filled with period detail. The bookstall is busy,
the well-dressed men and women all wear
hats, as was the norm, and in the foreground a
young boy clutches his fishing rod.

The Station, Scarborough.

◄ Postcards of stations are
popular, offering an insight
into a specific period of
time and, often, a lost world.
Scarborough station looks
much the same today, but gone
are the trams and the elegant
ladies with long summer
dresses, straw hats
and parasols seen in this
Edwardian view.

▼ Unlike the view at Carlisle
on the previous page, this is
a busy scene in 1965, and the
trainspotter in the foreground
is spoilt for choice. Near him,
a Class 47 diesel is making
a smoky start, while on the
opposite platform an LMS
Jubilee No. 45608, 'Gibraltar',
(lacking its nameplates) is being
attended to by its crew. Beyond
that is a DMU.

▶ Most seats are taken in the waiting room at Darlington in this 1973 view, taken by a British Rail photographer who perhaps had time on his hands. Everyone sits well wrapped up, clearly resigned to waiting for some time. The girl with the newspaper is reading about Richard Nixon's visit to Disneyland.

RIVERSIDE STATION, LIVERPOOL.

▲ This LNWR Official Card shows a busy scene at Liverpool's Riverside station, which was built to serve the North Atlantic liners. This American special to Euston is taking on passengers who have just arrived on one of the great ships of the time, perhaps the *Olympic* or *Mauretania*.

▶ Middlesbrough had a magnificent Gothic station, as seen on this Edwardian card. Completed in 1877, it was one of the town's best buildings. It survives, albeit somewhat reduced in scale by German bombing in World War II.

RAILWAY STATION, MIDDLESBROUGH.

Published by W. ALLAN, The Library, MIDDLESBROUGH.

▲ Railways were often affected by floods, and photographs showing the tracks between the platforms turning into a river are not unusual. This is at Cullercoats, near Tynemouth, probably early in the 20th century. Two men gaze gloomily at the photographer, one holding a shunter's pole he has used to check the water's depth.

▶ It is May 1974 and assorted passengers move across the platform at Penrith station, ready to board the London train that is pulling in, hauled by a Class 86 electric locomotive. In the distance a porter, in those days still a regular member of the station staff, struggles with two heavy suitcases.

◀ Something has drawn plenty of people to the platform at Blackburn on a sunny day in the 1960s. Many seem to be mothers with their children, casually dressed and clearly waiting for a particular train to arrive or for something to happen. Among them are a few passengers whose more formal dress reflects the normal life of the station.

▼ A Ford pulls away from a deserted-looking Ashton Charlestown station on a quiet day in the early 1960s. Sited near Stalybridge on a complex tangle of lines northwest of Manchester, the station, built in two-tone brick, was originally part of the Lancashire & Yorkshire network.

▶ Workington, now a rather battered station on the scenic Cumbrian Coast line, was, until 1966, the terminus of the line from Penrith across the Lake District via Keswick. This postcard view, with its curiously random scattering of people, shows the station in its better days.

STATION APPROACH, WORKINGTON.

9107/W2   SANKEYS

▶ Everything is in good order and tidy at Amotherby station, near Malton, but it looks as if nothing much happens there. The goods shed is shut and the porter's trolleys are parked casually on the platform. Two passengers are waiting, one in the sun and one in the shade, in this timeless scene on a line that closed to passengers in 1931 and to freight in 1964.

▼ In another timeless scene a porter walks to pick up a parcel left by the guard on the departing Whitby West Cliff train. Staithes station is otherwise deserted on a sunny day. Even the camping coach in the siding seems unoccupied, despite the well-known appeal of this famous stretch of coastline.

COACH

STAITHES

◄ Swinging his tea can in his hand and looking back towards the station building, the driver, his duties over, walks away from his old tank locomotive and its ancient single carriage, still marked ER. It is the late 1940s on the remote Easingwold branch in North Yorkshire and there seem, as so often, to be no passengers for the next journey along the 2½-mile line to Alne.

► Beck Holes, or Beckhole, was a minor halt on the original line from Whitby to Pickering. It was bypassed by a deviation line in 1865, but the original route remained open for freight. Between 1908 and 1914 a limited passenger service operated during the summer months. This presumably shows the arrival of the first of these holiday specials in 1908. The line is now part of the preserved North York Moors Railway.

ARRIVAL OF FIRST CAR AT BECK HOLE

◄ Airmyn & Rawcliffe was a surprisingly substantial and rather elegant timber station to the south of Selby. By the 1950s, when this photograph was taken, it was little used, though still in good order and smartly painted. A solitary member of staff stands on the broad wooden platform checking the waiting train, while another young man peers from the ticket office, watching the photographer.

Oxenholme to Windermere

When the Lancaster & Carlisle Railway reached Oxenholme in 1846, the people of Kendal felt left out and aggrieved. They therefore promoted their own 10-mile branch line, the Kendal & Windermere Railway, which was completed in 1847. In the process they invoked the wrath of local poet William Wordsworth, who, fearful that his beloved Lakeland was going to be desecrated, wrote a strongly worded sonnet ranting against the railway. This early example of nimbyism notwithstanding, and despite erratic time-keeping, the line was soon successful. It established Windermere, which at that time was no more than a small hamlet called Birthwaite some distance above the lake, as a popular resort.

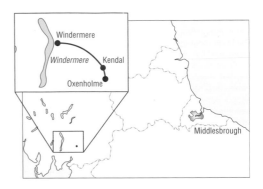

From the station, a handsome building in Lakeland stone with a porte cochère and a glazed roof, the town spread down to the lakeside, a classic example of a railway creating a resort out of very little. As traffic expanded, so the station grew to match it, with ever-lengthening platforms to handle the

▶ In 1907 Windermere station was a grand place, already much extended by the L&NWR to fulfil the needs of the many specials that brought thousands of visitors to this Lakeland gateway. The photographer has picked a quiet moment during the afternoon to capture the atmosphere of the station. The bookstall, with its stocks of newspapers, magazines and Frith's popular photographs of Lakeland scenery, is ready for the next wave of excited travellers.

holiday excursions that came from all over Britain. By 1879 the mighty L&NWR was in control, and the line continued to thrive through the LMS period and into the time of British Railways. As late as 1965, a scheduled named train, the Lakes Express, ran direct to Windermere from London. All this came to an end in the 1970s with the completion of the full electrification of the West Coast main line. From then on, Windermere was served by a shuttle service of diesel railcars, and the surroundings inevitably decayed as station buildings were taken out of use or closed. Windermere station, the gateway to the lakes, became notably run down, with only a single track still in use. This changed in the 1980s with the building of a new little station slightly to the north. Meanwhile, its grand Victorian predecessor became a supermarket, but managed to retain some of its original style.

▶ This L&NWR postcard, showing islands on Lake Windermere, was posted in London in November 1906. The message on the back is unusual: 'Splendid view of the King & Queen of Norway, the Prince and Princess of Wales and the Duke and Duchess of Connaught. Fortunately it remained fine for them.'

▶ Railway companies spent much time and effort promoting their resorts. The L&NWR was famous for its series of scenic view cards of places accessible via their services. This one shows the boat landing stage at Bowness. It offers 'delightful boating excursions and great sporting opportunities to anglers'.

BOATLANDING STAGE, BOWN...
L.&N.W. RAILWAY. LAKE WI...

▶ British Railways continued to promote Windermere and the Lake District as holiday destinations. This June 1961 leaflet, with its appealing drawing of a lake steamer, was designed to encourage the use of Holiday Runabout Tickets, which offered a wide range of journeys in the Lake District and along the Lancashire and Cumbrian coasts. The idea was 'an attractive form of Holiday Travel for passengers who wish to return to their own homes each day'. They could take their bicycles and their dogs, both of which cost the same as a child under 14, and they could travel on Windermere steamers.

PLEASE RETAIN THIS PROGRAMME FOR REFERENCE

HOLIDAY RUNABO
TICKETS
(GO AS YOU PLEASE)
AREA No. 2
LANCASHIRE COAS
and
LAKE DISTRICT

SECOND 30/- CLASS
CHILDREN UNDER 14, HALF FARE
TICKETS ARE NOT TRANSFERABLE

AVAILABLE FOR SIX DAYS
SUNDAY TO FRIDAY
30th JULY to 4th AUGUST 1961 (inclusive)
OR
6th AUGUST to 11th AUGUST 1961 (inclusive)
FROM
LIVERPOOL
AND STATIONS SHOWN HEREIN
Unlimited travel on any train between any stations within the area.

BICYCLE TICKETS 15/- DOG TICKETS 15/-
Issued in conjunction with the above

F.212

LONDON MIDLAND

ISLANDS ON LAKE WINDERMERE.
L.&N.W. RAILWAY.

The Windermere shuttle

Despite the many reminders of one-time glories, a journey to Windermere is still a classic branch line experience. Passengers for the branch leave the Virgin express at Oxenholme station and cross to the bay platform, where the shuttle service waits. The route as far as Kendal is a steady descent into the valley of the Kent, with splendid views of surrounding hills and fells, which rise to 2,000ft and more. Beyond Kendal and the crossing of the Kent, the line climbs to Burneside, a town famous for its paper mills. Until the 1960s these helped to maintain freight traffic on the branch. Next stop is Staveley, high above the village. In a landscape of increasing splendour, the line soon reaches its climax with a view ahead of the main Lake District peaks and ranges. From here, the train drops through fellside bracken and woodland towards the terminus at Windermere, with occasional glimpses far below of the lake and perhaps the boats that connect at Lakeside with the Lakeside & Haverthwaite preserved railway.

G. W. R.

WINDERMERE

▼ In the 1950s and early 1960s Windermere was still a busy station, with plenty of holiday specials filling the long platforms and a wide network of local services. The glazed train shed of the original station stands in the background, and on the right are goods sheds built from rough stone in a typical Lakeland style. Little of this can be seen today.

▲ After years of services in slightly decrepit diesel railcars, the Windermere branch now has smart new trains. Seen here in 2001, a Class 175 multiple unit is ready to depart from Windermere's minimalist station. The remains of the old station building, now a supermarket, stand in the background.

◄ A vehicle ferry still operates across the lake, linking Bowness on the eastern side with Sawrey, famous as the home of Beatrix Potter. This card shows the ferry in earlier days, carrying what seems to be a very fine 1930s touring car.

156. The ferry boat on Windermere.

Middlesbrough to Whitby

The Esk valley line from Middlesbrough to Whitby is today one of Britain's most famous branch lines, partly because of its history and the magnificence of its landscape, and partly because of its perennially uncertain future. Whenever there is a discussion about the viability of rural routes, this line is mentioned. At 35 miles, it is a long branch, and that is one of the problems. Maintenance is expensive, and traffic levels are unpredictable and hard to sustain. Also, it was never built as a branch. Until the 1960s the route was an integrated part of a whole network of lines, and Whitby itself was the meeting point of three busy railways.

Whitby's history is complex. First, in 1836, there was the Whitby & Pickering Railway, whose 24-mile line was initially partly worked by rope haulage. Next, after a long planning and building period, came the Whitby, Redcar & Middlesbrough Union's line from the north, opened in 1883. In 1885, after an equally long battle with finances and construction problems, the Scarborough & Whitby Railway's line from the south arrived.

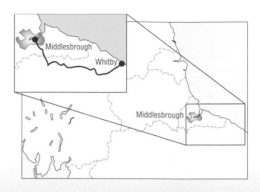

LONDON
NORTH EASTERN RAILWAY.
From _____ WHITBY

Grosmont

◄ It is the summer of 1971 and a diesel multiple unit carrying a group of rail enthusiasts pauses at Commondale, a station high in the North York Moors. Boarded up and disused, the station buildings retain their original lamps. Today this and other moorland stations are popular with walkers, and much has been done to promote walks that start from stations on the Middlesbrough to Whitby line.

► Hundreds of postcards celebrate the attractions of Whitby and its harbour, for the town has long appealed to visitors. The harbour, built on the estuary of the Esk, is a fine sight, framed by tiers of old buildings. A famous whaling port, it was also the starting point for Captain Cook's voyages of exploration. The popularity of Whitby jet jewellery put the town on the map in the 1800s, as did its association with Bram Stoker's *Dracula*.

Whitby Harbour.

◄ Larpool viaduct strides across the river Esk to the west of Whitby. It was built in 1885 to carry the railway south to Scarborough on a dramatic route along the coast. When this photograph, showing a local service on its way along the valley from Whitby, was taken in the early 1960s, the whole network was under threat. Today the line survives precariously, and the viaduct carries a footpath and cycleway.

Whitby, as a result, flourished, as a port and fishing centre, and as a place for tourists to visit. By the 1890s the North Eastern Railway was in control and in due course this became part of the LNER. From 1948 British Railways maintained the network, but by 1965 the supporting routes had closed and the Esk Valley line was left as a long and complicated branch. The section from Grosmont to Pickering has been preserved as the North Yorkshire Moors Railway.

Taking the Esk Valley line today

Initially, until it escapes the industry and suburbs of Middlesbrough, the journey is unremarkable. However, beyond Nunthorpe the North York Moors come into view, and the landscape continues to improve steadily as the train climbs to the 550ft level, reaching its summit on Kildale and Commondale moors. The train now drops down towards the Esk valley as the moors give way to woods and farmland, passing a series of stations serving remote hillside communities for whom the train is still the best way to go to school and work, and for shopping in town. In winter it is often the only way.

Following the Esk, the line criss-crosses the river, whose course is in some places through gentle fields and at others through wild ravines. At Grosmont the station is shared with the steam trains of the North Yorkshire Moors Railway. After more crossings of the Esk, at this point a substantial waterway, the train winds its way towards its destination along the north bank of the river. It passes beneath the great viaduct at

► A Class 101 diesel multiple unit pauses at Kildale in 1960, shortly after the introduction of these modern vehicles to the Whitby line. The open door might suggest that someone has misjudged the length of the platform and will have to make a jump for it. Today, Kildale is a moorland station popular with walkers, but the trains are much shorter and generally fit on to the platform.

▼ The Esk Valley line is for most people all about landscape, and many who use the line today take the train as the best way to enjoy the diversity of scenery that the line offers. Moorland, woods, river valleys and fantastic views are all part of this remarkable journey. Here, near Danby, the line follows the Esk through an old-fashioned landscape of small fields bounded by hedges, carpeting the hills with green. Old lanes follow the traditional field pattern, and the railway appears to be a natural part of the picture.

North Eastern Railway.

KNARESBRO.

From

WHITBY

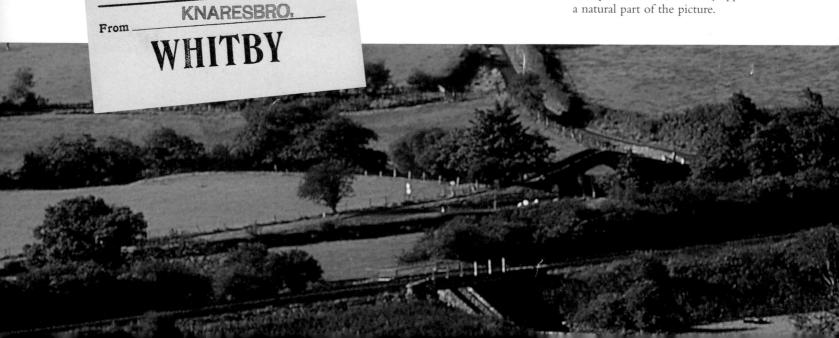

Larpool, which used to carry the line southwards to Scarborough, and then Whitby comes into view. The harbour and the tidal estuary are filled with small boats, while high above the town stand the red stone ruins of the abbey. It is a glorious end to a remarkable journey.

Town Stations

The major beneficiaries of the Victorian railway system in Britain were the small towns. Hitherto self-contained and relatively isolated, such places could now experience the benefits and pleasures of being part of an expanding national network. All over Britain, once the railways arrived, local industries thrived and people travelled. For this reason many towns became part of railway promotion schemes – some practical, some hopeless – into which large sums of local money were poured. These expressions of optimism are preserved in the names of countless early railway companies: the Leominster & Bromyard, the Callander & Oban, the Whitehaven, Cleator & Egremont, the Bishop's Stortford, Dunmow & Braintree, the Lewes &

▶ Cirencester, in Gloucestershire, had two stations and now has none. This is Cirencester Town, the GWR terminus at the end of the branch from Kemble, seen in 1959. It closed in 1964, but some of the buildings survive, indicating how well a local station could fit in with its surrounding architecture.

▼ Crewkerne station in Somerset was designed by Sir William Tite for the LSWR, following the pattern he established for that railway. Although reduced to one platform, it survives in reasonable condition and with adequate usage, despite being built a mile outside the town it serves.

Uckfield, the Mellis & Eye, the Bideford, Westward Ho! & Appledore, the Llanidloes & Newtown and many, many more, all conceived as independent local ventures. Other towns gained their railway connection through the ambitions of the big companies, and in some cases inter-company rivalry meant that a place ended up with two, or even three stations, offering different routes and connections. Most welcomed the railway with open arms, but there were those that did not, conspiring with local landowners to keep it at a distance. Usually, however, local pride, a desire to be part of the railway revolution and the ever-expanding schemes of the big companies combined to put small towns on the railway map.

▲ Another partial survivor is Keswick, in Cumbria, though the line was closed in 1972. Here, the end is near and the flags are out as passengers board the local for Penrith. It was opened in 1865 by the Cockermouth, Keswick & Penrith Railway.

All this was to come to an end with World War I and then the closures began, prompted initially by the spread of the motor bus and the loss of goods traffic. During the 1960s small towns across the country lost their railways. Those that survived the axe were often much diminished through changing social patterns and the impact of private road transport.

Many town stations reflected the economic and architectural ambitions of their creators and were as a result buildings that made an impact in their own local environment. In many cases those that survive still echo the optimism, and the investment, that brought them into being. Others are lingering ghosts of former grandeur, unable to adapt to the demands of a changed world. After a spell in the doldrums, many small town stations are now enjoying better times. Passengers have returned, and station buildings have been restored and are now an important part of the national railway heritage. Many have been listed, including some that closed long ago. Others have been

▲ Workington Main was, as its name implies, the town's most important station. It was once a busy place, reflecting the local industrial wealth, but by the autumn of 1993 it was a decaying ghost, with long overgrown platforms far beyond the reach of the little railcars on the Cumbrian Coast line.

▼ Thurso is Britain's northernmost station and, like its neighbour Wick, it still boasts the covered train shed built by the Sutherland & Caithness Railway in 1874 over its single platform. It was looking a bit sparse in 1994 when this photograph was taken but, remarkably, trains still come and go.

Midland Railway. P. F. 70.
R 2a.

HUNTINGDON

◀ Hawick, in the Scottish borders, benefited hugely from the arrival of the railway in 1849, and its textile industry flourished. The station was still busy in the Edwardian era, when this photograph was taken, but decline was steady from the 1930s and life finally came to an end in the 1960s.

lost, or replaced by smaller, modern structures that are easier to maintain. Overall, however, the small town station is something special, an individual and sometimes eccentric reflection of local dreams and ambitions, and its continued existence is a vital legacy – and a barrier against the onward march of uniformity.

▶ This 1911 postcard shows the Great Northern's station at Huntingdon, in Cambridgeshire, built in 1850 to give a small town a mainline connection. Until 1969 it was known as Huntingdon North, to distinguish it from the Great Eastern's Huntingdon East.

SCOTLAND

Station Scenes

The Scottish railway map was determined largely by geography. The main lines linking the primary cities were built quite quickly, followed by their local networks. Routes serving remoter regions, particularly in the north, were generally built later, and often at great expense, but the two main companies, the Caledonian and the Highland, were determined to build lines to serve as much of Scotland as possible. One of the results was a wealth of branch lines, most of which were lost in the 1950s and 1960s. Today, while most of the primary routes have survived, vast areas of Scotland are without any rail service. The real story is told, as ever, by photographs, and these show the diverse nature both of routes and stations.

NEW GALLOWAY STATION

▲ The main line to Stranraer via Castle Douglas was completed in 1862, and this became one of the primary routes for shipping services to Ireland. Stranraer is still a busy port, but it is now served by a roundabout route via Ayr. This is Stranraer Town station, on the line to Portpatrick, which closed in 1965.

▲ The Stranraer line passed through remote countryside for much of its route. Typical of the small, rural stations was New Galloway, seen here in the early 20th century with cars waiting to take visitors on tours around nearby Loch Ken.

◀ A smart stone station was built in the 1860s in Kirkcudbright, as the terminus for the branch line to the town from Castle Douglas. The line closed completely in 1965.

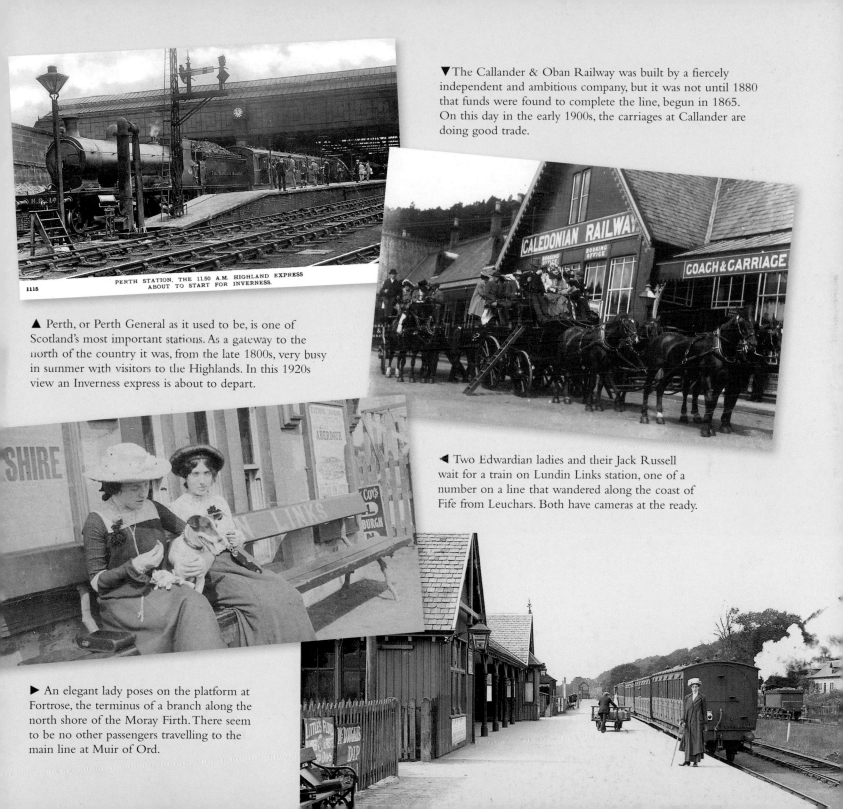

▼ The Callander & Oban Railway was built by a fiercely independent and ambitious company, but it was not until 1880 that funds were found to complete the line, begun in 1865. On this day in the early 1900s, the carriages at Callander are doing good trade.

PERTH STATION, THE 11.50 A.M. HIGHLAND EXPRESS ABOUT TO START FOR INVERNESS.

1115

▲ Perth, or Perth General as it used to be, is one of Scotland's most important stations. As a gateway to the north of the country it was, from the late 1800s, very busy in summer with visitors to the Highlands. In this 1920s view an Inverness express is about to depart.

◄ Two Edwardian ladies and their Jack Russell wait for a train on Lundin Links station, one of a number on a line that wandered along the coast of Fife from Leuchars. Both have cameras at the ready.

► An elegant lady poses on the platform at Fortrose, the terminus of a branch along the north shore of the Moray Firth. There seem to be no other passengers travelling to the main line at Muir of Ord.

▲ The glorious scenery around Killin station is apparent, but if the young man who is posing so casually in this 1967 photograph needs a train, he will have a long wait. The passenger service had ceased two years earlier.

▼ This 1920s view of Whistlefield Halt, north of Garelochhead, shows the splendour of its setting beside Loch Long. Today the line survives, but the station is long closed.

RAILWAY STATION, WHISTLEFIELD, LOCH LONG.

▲ Loch Tay, the terminus of the Killin branch, had not seen a passenger train for some years when this couple were photographed on the platform, perhaps in the 1950s, but the locomotive shed at Loch Tay, and therefore the line, remained in use until 1965.

◀ In this 1910 postcard, a North British Railway West Highland Express enters Glenfinnan station, on the line from Fort William to Mallaig. This rugged line, notable for the dramatic landscape and the nearby viaduct, had been completed only nine years earlier.

▼ Under the watchful eyes of two senior railwaymen and a member of Pitlochry's station staff, two trains cross. One is on track maintenance duties, and both are headed by Class 26 diesels. It is the early 1970s, when these locomotives were widely used throughout northern Scotland.

► In September 1960 an enthusiast and his friend, the photographer, have braved the weather and made the long journey on their motor scooters to Barcaldine Halt, on the Ballachulish branch from Connel Ferry. They have been lucky to see a veteran locomotive on duty.

◄ On a sunny May day in 1958, a special railtour organized by the Stephenson Locomotive Society has arrived at Lennoxtown, on the north Glasgow line from Kirkintilloch to Killearn. A couple of local girls, in summer frocks, have turned out to watch.

▲ In bright summer sunshine in August 1955, the branch line train from Dornoch to the mainline junction at The Mount rests at the platform while the driver has a cigarette break and his fireman loads coal into the grate. The carriage doors are open but there are no passengers. The line closed in 1960.

◄ Another branch that was little used in its later years ran to Aberfeldy from the main line at Ballinluig. Here, a couple of years before closure in 1965, the elderly tank locomotive and its single carriage wait while the station staff chat with the crew. There is not a passenger to be seen.

Glasgow to Oban

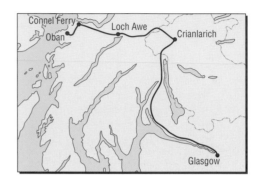

The railway to Oban was born out of the fierce competition between those two rival Scottish companies, the North British and the Caledonian. The battle was about opening up the west coast of the Highlands for tourism, freight and specialized local traffic such as fish. First on the scene was the Caledonian, through its backing of a small, independent railway, the Callander & Oban. Set up in 1865, this company was perennially short of money, so its line westwards from Callander was built in fits and starts. Services were finally opened to Oban in July 1880. Quickly successful, the railway did much to develop Oban as a modern resort. It also played a major role in promoting the popularity of Mull and the other islands accessible by steamers from Oban. For a few years the Callander & Oban, and thus the Caledonian, operated unchallenged, but the North British soon had its eye on this new source of traffic and in 1889 backed the setting up of the West Highland Railway. Opened throughout to Fort William in 1894, this expensive and heavily engineered line through a wild landscape linked Glasgow directly to the western Highlands for the first time. The two lines met at Crianlarich, but each company built its own station, and maintained a sense of independence. Later developments in the region by the North British and the Caledonian included the long branch to Mallaig from Fort William, opened in 1901, and the Ballachulish branch north along Loch Linnhe from Connel Ferry, a few miles outside Oban. Things remained the same until the 1960s, under LMS and then British Railways' control.

▼ Highland lines were almost invariably single track, to reduce construction costs of railways serving small populations in a challenging landscape. This modern view is typical, and timeless, giving a sense of the journey's visual excitement and colour.

▲ In 1960, steam was still dominant on the Oban line. Here, on a bright day, a train drifts across the more open landscape east of Taynuilt, overshadowed by Ben Cruachan. The role played by the railway in opening up an inaccessible landscape cannot be overstated.

◄ Big, locomotive-hauled trains were a feature of the Oban route until relatively recently, giving a sense of grandeur completely lost in the modern age of the diesel railcar. In 1961 two paired diesels haul a scheduled service along Glen Lochy.

The western Highlands did not escape the closures of the 1960s that devastated so much of Scotland's railway network. The Ballachulish branch closed in 1966, but the great steel-girder bridge across the entrance to Loch Etive survived, for use as a road. More significant was the obliteration of every line east of Crianlarich, severing the links to Dunblane and Perth. All that remained was the West Highland route from Glasgow to Fort William and Mallaig, and a fragment of the old Caledonian network in the form of a branch line from Crianlarich to Oban. A connection was made at Crianlarich to allow trains on the West Highland line to join the Oban branch, and the old Caledonian station, Crianlarich Lower, was abandoned. As a result, Oban services start from Glasgow.

Connel Ferry Bridge

A remarkable structure, and in many ways the most extraordinary piece of engineering built for any branch line in Britain, Connel Ferry bridge was designed in 1903 by Sir John Wolfe Barry. Its cantilever steel style is the same as the Forth rail bridge. Indeed, it was, when built, the largest single steel span in Britain after the Forth bridge. The design was determined by the need for high clearance above the water and by strong tidal currents that made it impossible to build supporting piers in the water. It was designed to carry a single-track railway and a very narrow road, but road vehicles were carried across on flat rail wagons until 1913. Even then, there was not enough room for trains and road vehicles to cross at the same time, so there was a complicated system of gates at each end. After the closure of the Ballachulish branch in 1966, the bridge became part of the A828 road.

The journey

The West Highland line is a spectacular journey, a long single-track route from Craigendoran, on the Clyde near Dumbarton, to Fort William. The route is through Faslane and then along the shores of Loch Long to Arrochar, and thence northwards by Loch Lomond. From here the line climbs to Crianlarich. The best part of the route is the section north of Crianlarich, through Bridge of Orchy and high across Rannoch Moor, but the southern part is not to be scorned, with a long sequence of fine vistas in colours typical of the Highlands. Notable also are the stations, built to a standard pattern, which echoes a Swiss chalet, and set on an island platform to allow trains to pass on the otherwise single track. The station buildings are exceptionally pretty, sometimes with matching signal box. This sequence of stylistically matching stations on one line is unique in Britain.

▼ Today, Connel Ferry bridge is a remarkable sight, clearly built as a railway bridge, even though it now carries road traffic. Always famously narrow, it is still single-tracked, with traffic-light control.

From Crianlarich westwards to Oban the route is distinctly different, although initially it runs parallel to the Fort William line, branching away along Glen Lochy only after Tyndrum, another spot with separate stations built by the rival companies. Woods and hills lead to Dalmally, which for a while – when the Callander & Oban's money ran out yet again – was the line's terminus. The line then flanks the northern shore of Loch Awe, offering a good view of the ruins of Kilchurn Castle. Next come the famous Falls of Cruachan, with Ben Cruachan dominating the landscape to the north. Narrow rock cuttings and dramatic scenery take the railway to Taynuilt and the shore of Loch Etive. Connel Ferry bridge soon comes into view, crossing the Falls of Lora at the mouth of Loch Etive. The railway now turns southwards and winds its way towards Oban through woods, with views of the town and its harbour. There is time to admire the sturdy Victorian architecture and the extraordinary version of Rome's

▼ In 1987, the year after Oban's splendid station was demolished, a Glasgow-bound train sets off, hauled by a Class 37 diesel locomotive, then one of the mainstays of Highland lines. McCaig's Tower, Oban's own Colosseum, stands on the hill.

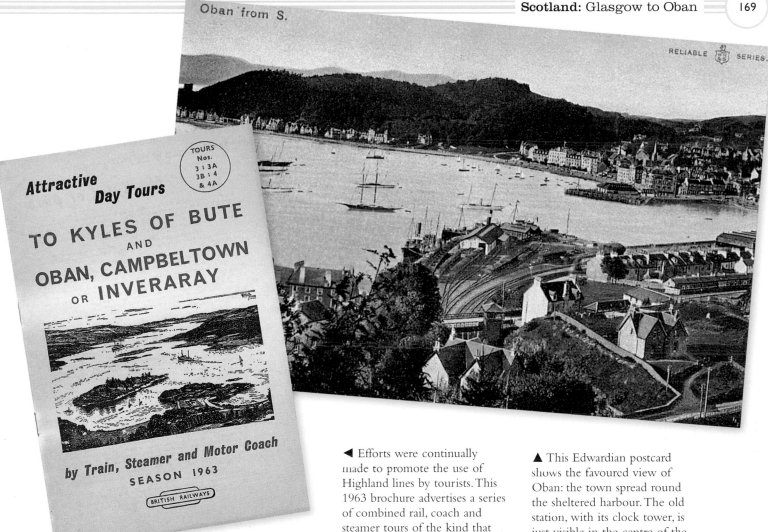

Oban from S.

RELIABLE SERIES.

Attractive Day Tours
TO KYLES OF BUTE
AND
OBAN, CAMPBELTOWN
OR INVERARAY
by Train, Steamer and Motor Coach
SEASON 1963
BRITISH RAILWAYS

TOURS
Nos.
3 : 3A
3B : 4
& 4A

◄ Efforts were continually made to promote the use of Highland lines by tourists. This 1963 brochure advertises a series of combined rail, coach and steamer tours of the kind that are still popular with visitors.

▲ This Edwardian postcard shows the favoured view of Oban: the town spread round the sheltered harbour. The old station, with its clock tower, is just visible in the centre of the card. The lines are filled with trains, and steamers wait at the quay to take passengers to Mull and other nearby islands. A row of big hotels reflects Oban's successful development by the railway from the 1880s.

Colosseum, called McCaig's Tower after the local philanthropist who commissioned it to ease local unemployment. Originally Oban had a memorable station, a gabled and elaborate Arts & Crafts structure, crowned by a French-style clock tower. It was entirely suitable for the resort town, a fitting climax to the journey, and it sheltered passengers waiting for ferries to the islands. It was demolished in 1986, to be replaced by an inappropriate redbrick edifice.

Fort William to Mallaig

At 41 miles long, the line from Fort William to Mallaig can hardly be called a branch, yet this westward extension of the West Highland route from Glasgow has all the important branch line characteristics. Fish was the inspiration for building a railway across the wild and inaccessible landscape of the western Highlands, and it was the battle for the fish trade between two Scottish railways, the Caledonian and the North British, that brought it into being. The railway reached Fort William in 1894, and it took another seven years, and a huge expenditure, to extend it to Mallaig. The heavily engineered route includes countless rock cuttings, steep gradients and viaducts, and eleven tunnels.

For some time fish and freight fulfilled the line's expectations, and passenger carrying was almost a secondary consideration. However, since the 1950s the line has in effect been a railway 'Road to the Isles' and has had to rely increasingly on tourism. Today, the emphasis is on the journey itself, rather than the destination, with the train being seen as a mobile viewing platform that makes its way through some of Scotland's most awe-inspiring scenery. It also passes through a region closely associated with Bonny Prince Charlie and the 1745 Jacobite rebellion. It was at Glenfinnan on 19 August 1745 that the clans declared themselves for the prince and the Stuart cause. It was the pursuit of tourists that inspired British Railways to introduce the scheduled steam-hauled trains on the Mallaig line in the late 1980s. These services proved highly successful and, now marketed as 'The Jacobite', they continue to operate in the summer months.

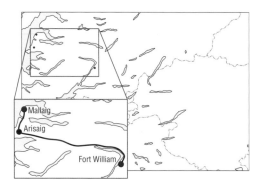

▼ In a magnificently wild and snowy landscape, a steam train crosses the 21 arches of Glenfinnan viaduct. Built on a curve, this pioneering concrete structure is a favourite with photographers. It is 1987, the start of regular steam-hauled services on the line, and a Stanier Black Five is setting the pace for the future.

EVENING LIGHT OVER BEN NEVIS FROM CORPACH.

▼ The impetus for building the line to Mallaig over such hard terrain was the desire to capture some of the fish traffic, a major source of income for railways until the 1950s. A busy fishing harbour before the coming of the railway, Mallaig expanded rapidly after 1901. This 1920s card, 'The Morning Catch', shows fish being auctioned prior to packing for transport by train.

▲ 'Evening light over Ben Nevis from Corpach' is the title of this early postcard, a typically romantic view of the great mountain that towers above Fort William and the line to Mallaig, which passes through Corpach. It is a glorious scene, enlivened by the little boat in the foreground.

8058. THE MORNING CATCH, MALLAIG, INVERNESS-SHIRE.

One of the greatest railway journeys in the world

The route is a continual series of excitements, from the start in Fort William under the shadow of Ben Nevis to the finish at Mallaig, with views over the fishing boats in the harbour to the islands beyond. In between is the crossing of the Caledonian Canal on the famous 1901 swing-bridge, the delightful run alongside the shore of Loch Eil, the climb into the mountains for the crossing of the Glenfinnan viaduct and the views of Loch Shiel. Then comes the twisting route along the rocky valley of the river Ailort to Lochailort, the Atlantic views across the bays of Loch Nan Uamh, the inland journey through woods to Arisaig and finally the sandy beaches of Morar. The Mallaig section of the West Highland line is often promoted as one of the great railway journeys of the world. On a sunny day when the train and the landscape are bathed in that special and ever-changing Scottish light and colour, that claim is certainly justified.

▼ On a glorious spring day in 1988, a dirty Class 37 diesel locomotive, in late British Rail colours, trundles its two-coach train past Loch Eil, on the way to Mallaig, through scenery that makes this one of the world's most exciting rail journeys.

▶ Fort William station in the 1950s was a busy place, with plenty of freight and passenger activity, including the nightly sleepers to and from London. Here, a former LNER K2 locomotive stands on the quayside while passers-by pay more attention to whatever is going on in the harbour. Still standing then was the old station, an eccentric stone-built structure with a spire, a tower, a steeply pitched roof and a big lunette window over the entrance. This was all demolished in 1975.

◀ Mallaig is another stone-built station, but more in the manner of a house with gables. This 1974 photograph shows well the generous platform awnings, since removed. The Class 27 locomotive is reversing its rake of carriages out of the platform, on the way to the carriage sidings, where they will be prepared for the journey back to Fort William.

▶ Apart from steam services and specials, long, locomotive-hauled trains are a thing of the past on the Mallaig line. Today, services are operated by the ubiquitous sprinters. A typical example is seen here in the early days of privatization. All around the station are overgrown reminders of better days.

INDEX

Note: page numbers in **bold** refer to information contained in captions.

PICTURE CREDITS

Unless otherwise specified, all archive photographs and ephemera are from either the author's or the publisher's collection.

l=left; r=right; t=top; b=bottom; m=middle

Photographs by Paul Atterbury: 29mr; 31tr; 50t; 76tr; 93bl; 152
DA Anderson: 55t
Ben Ashworth: 28/29t; 30b; 79tr; 86t; 105r
JH Aston: 40tl
Hugh Ballantyne: 12tl; 21tr; 27tl; 52br
RB Barr: 89ml
Harold D Bowtell: 149tl

Ian Burgum/Burgum Boorman Ltd: 18b; 19bl; 69r; 118/119b; 150/151b; 173br
HC Casserley: 87bl; 126b; 128b; 132tl
RM Casserley: 16tl; 111tl
CRL Coles: 33ml
Colour-Rail: 44/45b; 46b; 51b; 68b; 96b; 98l; 124/125b; 146b; 148b; 151t; 173tr
Derek Cross: 106; 138br
Hugh Davies: 83b
Mike Esau: 47t; 101br
TG Flanders: 17b
PJ Fowler: 14tr; 15t
C Gammell: 39bl; 113b; 137t; 162b
JG Glover: 54b
John Goss: 78b; 86b; 173ml
L Hanson: 84t; 88tl
Tony Harden: 10tr; 11tl; 11tr; 11br; 12mr; 12bl; 13tr; 13ml; 14tl; 14b; 17tr; 38br; 40bl; 41tr; 42bl; 43tl; 63tl; 64ml; 65tr; 65ml; 66tr; 112ml; 114tr; 114br; 139tr;

139br; 141tl; 141mr; 143mr; 155br; 158t; 158mr; 158bl; 159tl; 159tr; 159ml; 159br; 160mr; 160bl; 163bl
JC Haydon: 38tr; 41b; 42t; 162t
GT Heavyside: 87t; 140b
Julian Holland: 33br; 74b; 76tl; 121b; 122tr; 124tr; 154b; 154/155t; 164b; 166/167
AC Ingram: 115b
Alan Jarvis: 72b; 78mr; 129t; 133b; 153t
MA Jose: 84b
MA King: 30/31t
Locomotive & General Photographic: 70tr; 104t
Michael Mensing: 85tl; 91tr; 93tr; 101t; 165tl; 165tr
Brian Morrison: 71b
Gavin Morrison: 25b; 27b; 29bl; 59b; 91b; 102b; 105l; 107t; 116b; 119t; 132b; 147t; 170/171b
G Newall: 114tl

J Osgood: 82br
RB Parr: 160t
Ivo Peters Collection: 73tr; 92b
GA Richardson: 94bl
RC Riley: 23t; 28bl; 31br; 53t; 56br; 66b; 94/95t; 127t; 130t
Bill Robertson: 161b
John Scrace: 32b
Brian Sharpe: 77bl; 103t; 168b; 172b
NC Simmons: 65b
Andrew Swift: 21b; 22tl; 22b; 26mr; 26bl; 77br; 100b; 127b; 131b; 144b; 155ml
Douglas Thompson: 111br; 129b; 142t
The Transport Treasury (RC Riley): 122b
Steve Turner: 136b
RE Tustin: 24mr
IL Wright: 63tr

A DAVID & CHARLES BOOK

© F&W Media International, Ltd 2013

F&W Media International, Ltd is a subsidiary of F+W Media, Inc
10151 Carver Road, Suite #200, Blue Ash, OH 45242, USA

First published in the UK in 2013
Copyright © Paul Atterbury 2013

Paul Atterbury has asserted his right to be identified as author of this work in accordance with the Copyright, Designs and Patents Act, 1988.

Entries in this publication were originally published in the following titles: *Tickets Please!*, *Branchline Britain*, *Along Country Lines* and *Life Along the Line*.

The publisher has endeavoured to contact all contributors of pictures for permission to reproduce. If there are any errors or omissions please notify the publisher in writing.

All rights reserved. No part of this publication may be reproduced, stored in a retrieval system, or transmitted, in any form or by any means, electronic or mechanical, by photocopying, recording or otherwise, without prior permission in writing from the publisher.

A catalogue record for this book is available from the British Library.

ISBN-13: 978-1-4463-0299-6
ISBN-10: 1-4463-0299-7

Printed in China RR Donnelley for:
F&W Media International, Ltd
Brunel House, Forde Close, Newton Abbot, TQ12 4PU, UK

10 9 8 7 6 5 4 3 2 1

Publisher: Ali Myer
Junior Acquisitions Editor: Verity Graves-Morris
Proofreader: Stuart Robertson
Junior Art Editor: Jodie Lystor
Junior Designer: Jennifer Stanley
Production Manager: Beverley Richardson

F+W Media publishes high quality books on a wide range of subjects.
For more great book ideas visit: www.fwmedia.co.uk